COMMUNITY, EMPOWERMENT
AND SUSTAINABLE
DEVELOPMENT

SUR
COUNTY

COMMUNITY, EMPOWERMENT AND SUSTAINABLE DEVELOPMENT

Edited by John Blewitt

The Converging World Series
from the Schumacher Institute

First published in the UK in 2008
by Green Books Ltd,
Foxhole, Dartington,
Totnes, Devon TQ9 6EB

The Converging World Series is a project of The Schumacher Institute
Bush House, Prince Street, Bristol BS1 4HU
www.schumacherinstitute.org.uk

Text printed on 100% recycled paper
Colour section and covers made for 80% recycled material

Printed by TJ International, Padstow, Cornwall, UK

ISBN 978 1 900322 31 7

Contents

Acknowledgements

Many people and communities have directly and indirectly contributed to this book. There are many whose names are unknown but whose experiences and aspirations are in effect the subject of this text. More specifically, the work of the Schumacher Institute, John Elford and the staff at Green Books, and the generosity of John Pontin have been central to the realisation of this project. Thanks must also go to my wife, Lorna Blewitt, for designing the front cover.

The intention is for this book series to illustrate the need for and exemplify possibilities of *The Converging World*.

List of contributors

Dr Cletus Babu was born on 12th October 1952 in a fisher village called Puthenkadai to his loving parents, namely Soosaiyan and Savariapillai. From an early age he started developing the skills and character traits necessary to be a good and committed social worker. The thirst for serving the poor and marginalised made him leave the priesthood and start the developmental organisation 'Social Change And Development' (SCAD) in 1985. Integrated development of the poor and marginalised is SCAD's vision, and he has led the delivery of quality services in formal and non-formal education, health, community organisation and community development in the backward region of Southern Tamil Nadu in India. A team of committed social workers formed and trained by him help in his mission of educating and empowering the poorest people in 453 drought-prone and undeveloped villages. He is pleased to share the development experience of SCAD with readers, and is grateful to *The Converging World*, John Pontin and Dr John Blewitt for offering this opportunity of doing so.

John Blewitt is Sustainability and Knowledge Transfer Co-ordinator and co-director of the MSc in Sustainable Development in the School of Geography, Archaeology and Earth Resources at the University of Exeter. He has extensive experience of adult, further and higher education, community development and media communications. He is a member of the IUCN Commission on Communication and Education, an adviser to WWF International on the *One Planet Leaders* programme, and a member of the UK Sustainable Development Panel and Sustainability South West. He is a Fellow of the Higher Education Academy, co-editor of *The Sustainability Curriculum* (Earthscan, 2004), and author of *The Ecology of Learning* (Earthscan, 2006) and *Understanding Sustainable Development* (Earthscan, 2008). He is editor of the Converging World series, published by Green Books.

Abdullahi Haji-Abdi has over 15 years experience working as a volunteer Community Developer with the Somali Diaspora in London. His main interest is community leadership, with emphasis on sustainability and the role of education in improving the quality of services offered by Somali

Community Projects. After completing the MSc in Education for Sustainability course in LSBU, he is now attending a Professional Doctorate in Education which has a focus on Equality, Diversity and Sustainability.

Kaz Janowski has been a radio producer at the BBC World Service since 1996, where he has made programmes on science, literature and history and programmes teaching English. Before joining the BBC he was a teacher of English as a Foreign Language in Poland, Malaysia, Kuwait and the UK for 15 years, following a degree in Biology at the University of Sussex and postgraduate research in Biology at the Jagiellonian University, Krakow, Poland.

Monica Janowski is a lecturer in Social Anthropology at the University of Sussex. She has carried out research among the Kelabit of Borneo and the Polish immigrant community in the UK; among her publications is *The Forest, Source of Life: the Kelabit of Sarawak,* published by the British Museum Press in 2003. She has worked on numerous international development research projects with natural and social scientists from institutions in the UK and other countries in the North and the South. Since 1997 she has collaborated with Kaz on making ten radio series for the BBC World Service and for local radio stations in Africa on topics related to international development.

Nicola Jones has worked for 18 years as a private client, tax and corporate lawyer in London and Bermuda. Since leaving Bermuda she has worked as a family business and family wealth adviser, relationship counsellor and lecturer. Her time is now spent principally working for the Schumacher Institute for Sustainable Systems, The Converging World and completing her MA in Gender Studies at the School of Oriental and African Studies, London.

Donna Ladkin is Senior Lecturer in Organisational Learning and Leadership at Cranfield School of Management, where she directs the School's 'Leading for Sustainability' programme. She has a background in organisational behaviour and environmental philosophy, disciplines which inform both her teaching and research in the areas of business ethics, organisations and sustainability, and philosophical approaches to leadership.

Mr G. Nagarajan is an experienced social worker, having gained a degree in science and a diploma in social work, and undertaken an intensive course in General Management Practices and Income-Generating enterprises at University of Cranfield School of Management, United Kingdom. Besides his broad educational qualifications, he has rich experience in the field of empowerment education and different areas of social work. Presently he is the team leader for the SCAD's Social Work Program, and has been deeply involved with the tsunami-hit people in the development initiatives led by the Village Development Councils (VDC) in the backward districts of Tirunelveli and Tuticorin in Tamil Nadu, India.

Betty Okot completed her MSc in Education for Sustainability at London South Bank University in 2007, and she is currently a Tutor on the EfS programme. Her interests in development and sustainability issues link with her experience of working in the civil society, secondary and higher education sectors in Africa and the UK. Betty's familiarity with the various sectors engendered in her the drive to gain more knowledge of the growing global imbalances and the need to become an agent of change. Betty has since been involved in policy and research-related areas of work, mainly with Diaspora organisations in the UK. Her article 'Here and There', featured in the September 2007 edition of the Network by the British Overseas NGOs for Development (BOND), was an important expression of why development should be inclusive. The article is also a testament to her deep insight into how the Diaspora groups practise development.

Siobhan Riordan is a part-time Senior Lecturer in the School for Social Sciences at the University of East London. She is founder of the first postgraduate programme in women's leadership in the UK and the first BA in Social Enterprise in Europe. Her academic studies include women's organisations, community health, civil society and NGO development. She also runs her own private consultancy firm providing training for local government, police and health agencies in partnership development and community engagement. She is a trained Psychosexual Therapist and group-work facilitator, with over 30 years experience in social entrepreneurship and community development.

Ian Roderick holds Master's degrees in Operational Research and in Responsibility and Business Practice. He was co-founder of a successful software company and can now devote his time and energy equally to The Converging World and to the Schumacher Institute for Sustainable Systems. He is the current president of the UK Systems Society and a Fellow of the RSA.

David Selby is Professor of Education for Sustainability and Director of the Centre for Sustainable Futures at the University of Plymouth. He was previously (1992-2003) Professor of Education and Director of the International Institute for Global Education at the Ontario Institute for Studies in Education of the University of Toronto, Canada. He has directed UN-funded and orchestrated curriculum development projects in some ten countries in south-east Europe, the Middle East and Central Asia, and has lectured or facilitated workshops and seminars in global education, environmental education, education for sustainability and related fields in more than thirty countries. He has (co)written or (co)edited some twenty books and over one hundred book chapters and articles including latterly some path-finding papers on climate change and education for sustainability. Recent articles have appeared in the *Journal of Geography in Higher Education* and the *International Journal on Innovation and Sustainable Development*. His books include *Global Teacher, Global Learner* (1988), *Earthkind: A Teachers' Handbook on Humane Education* (1995), *In the Global Classroom, Books One* and *Two* (1999, 2000), and *Weaving Connections: Educating for Peace, Social and Environmental Justice* (2000). His most recent book is *Green Frontiers: Environmental Educators Dancing Away from Mechanism* (Rotterdam, Sense, 2008). He was the co-recipient of the Canadian Peace Education Award in 2003. He has both British and Canadian nationality.

Lucy Thompson is currently working as a freelance consultant in Sustainability, most recently having undertaken a research project for Global Action Plan into corporate behaviour change. Since graduating from her first degree in Philosophy and Politics in 1998 she has worked in a variety of areas, including publishing and as a researcher at The Scottish Parliament. Lucy lived and worked as a volunteer on an Emmaus community in south-west France in 2003. She completed an MSC in Sustainable Development at Exeter University in 2008.

Ros Wade is Reader in Education at London South Bank University and co-director of the MSc Education for Sustainability.

Foreword

by John Pontin

This series of books carries the title of 'The Converging World', which is the name given to an organisation created in 2007 to tackle what many people call the century of crises – the seemingly overwhelming issues of climate change, the end of the oil age, the scarcity of water, food and raw materials, unstable financial systems and a host of consequent problems all due to the inherent divergent processes in our global society that lead to greater and greater inequality.

The Converging World (TCW) is a social enterprise that uses the ideas of contraction and convergence to reduce the differences in resource use, wealth, and impact on the environment between the rich and the poor, and between the free and the suppressed. It directly affects the twin issues of climate change and peak oil by investing in renewable energy in countries like India and then using the two streams of revenue, from electricity and carbon credits, to pay for projects that will see a convergence happen across all nations.

TCW is greatly concerned to work with and for community action. The issues we face are not a matter for governments to solve alone – the activities of millions of people working within their communities is essential as well. The groundswell of change is encouraging, but it needs nurturing, and needs resources. What better way could there be than for the rich communities in the world to find those resources from within their own peoples, to use them to make the structural changes necessary to adapt, like the transition to post-oil, and to invest their wealth with poor communities – those that are struggling to create new, thriving and sustainable economies?

Of course this 'century of crises' is immensely complex, and demands an openness of minds to comprehend and to devise practical ways forward. As the British Prime Minister recently said, "It is time to reimagine international institutions and build a truly global society." This is leadership to produce the top-down changes, and if that is coupled with grassroots efforts to reimagine what is possible from the bottom up, then we will find ways to subdue and tame the forces that lead to such profligate use of the Earth's resources and the grotesque differences of wealth, health, rights and opportunities.

I am sure that this series of books will contribute to the reimagining, the rethinking, required. They will cover a wide range of subjects crossing intellectual boundaries, but always with the pursuit of quality as the goal – quality of living, quality of our experience of this lonely and vulnerable planet, and quality of our responsibility to others.

John Pontin OBE
2008

Introduction

by John Blewitt

The overall themes of this book are those of community, empowerment and connectedness. If sustainable development means anything, it means living within the ecological carrying capacity of our planet, and doing so in peace and harmony. Despite our manifest cultural, economic, social, ethnic and historical differences, we human beings can only cease exploiting the planet and its wonderful richness if we cease exploiting and harming ourselves. Indeed, in harming the Earth we do harm ourselves. We have become our own worst enemies, but we are also our best hope of transcending the disasters we have visited upon ourselves. We have created our problems as well as the differences we sometimes find so confusing and threatening. We must therefore learn to address these challenges by celebrating the vibrancy and excitement engendered by the Earth's biological and cultural diversity. We must learn new ways of securing our future by nurturing economic and social well-being in an ecologically sensitive manner. To do this, we need to learn from and about each other, to fully understand the implications of our relationships with the planet. Consequently, this book offers a small contribution to understanding the necessary process of sustainable development by enabling a variety of voices to be heard, perspectives to be viewed and stories to be told.

As the first book in a projected series supporting The Converging World (TCW), it is fitting that Chapter One has been written by two people at the core of TCW, Ian Roderick and Nicola Jones, who outline the aims, objectives and history of TCW. Rooted in systems thinking, TCW has an intriguing complexity that in its practical outcomes is both simple and practical, benefiting communities as far apart as north Somerset in the United Kingdom to coastal villages in Tamil Nadu in southern India. Quality of life, economic well-being and financial investment in sustainable energy sources are central to the 'win-win' possibilities TCW offers.

What is perhaps truly innovative and encouraging is that individuals, groups, businesses and others do not need to wait for governments to take the lead or give permission. TCW connects communities and empowers individuals through its values and actions. In Chapter Two, Siobhan Riordan's attention is drawn to the practical issues surrounding climate change adaptation in Africa and the important role of non-government organisations. The emphasis is again on community and empowerment. She notes: "The localised nature of adaptation makes it of particular relevance for Africa, because the majority of people live in rural villages. Protecting these rural populations from climate change impacts requires a village-level approach." Climate change adaptation also requires serious engagement with socio-economic inequalities, cultural difference, gender, politics and power as much as, or perhaps rather than, any technical fix or external economic intervention that may be in the offing. Combining climate initiatives with sustainable development leads to an enlightening discussion of carbon markets, with the author concluding that carbon trading is highly ineffective at reducing greenhouse gas emissions and "is opening up new income flows for sustainable development and adaptation projects". These are often led by NGOs who crucially "create the infrastructure and technical support necessary to facilitate access and participation of villages and small communities in carbon trading".

David Selby's contribution (Chapter Three) explores global education as "sustainable community education". Drawing on a wealth of experience as a professional educator and having a deep commitment to learning as a fundamental element of sustainability, Selby begins his discussion with a theoretical overview that explores conceptual meanings and empirical practices. Being asked to define the essence of global education, Selby does so eloquently and succinctly, and then goes on to show how it plays out in Brazil, the Middle East and Albania. These areas have not been without their differences and conflicts, and too often citizens of other parts of the world know only of this thanks to the international news media's abiding interest in war and discord. For Selby, however, dialogue, participation and interaction are central to an empowering, connecting and liberating educational practice. This concern with learning and education is further developed in Chapters Four and Five, written by Dr Cletus Babu, founder and director of the grassroots NGO SCAD (Social Change And Development), and Mr G. Nagarajan, the team leader for SCAD's Social Work Program in Tamil Nadu, southern India. These chapters demonstrate the intense commitment informing SCAD's energy and achievements in an environment that offers more than its fair share of difficulties, challenges and problems. TCW has close relationships with SCAD, as Roderick and Jones explained, but here it is the direct empowerment of women, the education of young people, the democratic participation of village communities in development policies and actions, initiatives designed to improve lives and livelihoods, the barriers to development imposed by the caste system and the fearsome challenges presented by the destruction wrought by the massive tsunami of December 2004 that are highlighted by Dr Babu and Mr Nagarajan.

Following Nagarajan's discussion of nature and its power, it is fitting perhaps that Donna Ladkin in Chapter Six reflects on our relationships with the natural world, and by extension with other people. By exploring elements from her own personal life story, particularly her childhood in northern Maine, she then elegantly turns to the ideas and insights of two Western philosophers, Maurice Merleau-Ponty and Martin Heidegger. Ladkin questions whether we are in fact correct in conceptually separating ourselves from 'nature'. We are actually part of it: all of us – wherever we are, whoever we are and whenever we have lived, live or will live. To see this is to recognise that we must learn to live again by grounding ourselves, by reinhabiting the world which we have plundered and abused. She writes: "Reinhabitation – dwelling, if you will, provides the means for coming to know our place among the more-than-human world, and through a direct experience of that interconnection, can foster a (literally!) grounded sense of well-being". And it is groundedness of various sorts that runs through the next three chapters. Lucy Thompson uses her experience of having been a volunteer in an Emmaus community as the basis for her discussion in Chapter Seven of a relatively little-known but significant development project. After fifty years Emmaus is a global network with roots still very much in individual and community needs. The twin emphases of Emmaus are community and dignity. The organisation helps a wide range of disadvantaged, disaffected and sometimes broken people through offering hope, work, shelter, community and purpose. Many Emmaus communities are now developing a clear commitment to environmental as well as social sustainability. Through its international network it had been able to create "a web of solidarity" where "the true value of the individual can be realised". Chapter Eight explores the experiences, needs and activities of diaspora communities in the United Kingdom. Again drawing on direct experience, Abdullahi Haji-Abdi and Betty Okot present two detailed case studies illustrating attempts to bridge community divisions and build a sense of shared identity. The African Community Development Foundation (ACDF) and the London Somali community offer some object lessons in learning to live in a globalised world where mobility and change are often forced and sometimes violent. What comes through this chapter is the absolute necessity of co-operation, connectivity and participation as the basis for an empowering community practice that clearly recognises rather than suppresses or avoids difference. "It is a world where you have to get on with life," Haji and Okot state, but it is also a world where there is much to learn from hardships and struggles: "The skills which are so crucial to diaspora communities – of adaptation, resilience, conflict resolution, self-empowerment – will be essential for all of us if we are to create a just and sustainable future for humankind." Too true.

In Chapter Nine, Monica and Jaz Janowski examine the power of radio with a "dose of passion". It is important for the mass media to be used by communities who are themselves the targeted audiences. Community members must learn to create their own messages and present them, with the help of those who have the requisite technical skills, so they can be heard, listened to, understood and acted upon. Food security, health and nutrition are of paramount importance in many majority world countries, and Monica and Jaz Janowski offer a perceptive discussion of development communication projects in Africa ending with suggestions concerning how future communication and research can ensure educational and behavioural change objectives interface more effectively with local cultures and perceptions. In the final chapter, I look at how the moving image and the internet provide new opportunities for connectedness, community and empowerment. The worldwide web provides unparalleled communication opportunities for increasing numbers of groups and organisations to be both producers and consumers. The internet is quickly becoming the space where we can see and enter into the lives of others, and digital video is the means by which we can communicate the future while we create it. However, what we do with the new and emerging media technologies, or are allowed to do with them by governments and large corporations, will in large part influence these conditions of possibility. But . . . to build resilience, develop skills, celebrate difference, trade in carbon, see other people's worlds, hear the voices of others and peer into the future, we need to harness and exploit the potential opportunities for connectedness these new technologies afford. It is possible.

Devon

July, 2008

Chapter One

The Converging World

by Ian Roderick with Nicola Jones

This Converging World Series will comprise both edited and single-authored books that will act as guides to ideas, values and experiences of linking people across many divides, whether of geography, culture, religion or simple opportunities to lead fulfilling lives. The series has arisen to accompany the growth of a new charity called The Converging World which provides for education, poverty alleviation and environmental protection. Its objectives are:

- To reduce carbon dioxide (or equivalent) emissions to lessen global warming and the impact of climate change.
- To seek worldwide convergence of resource use and wealth.
- To demonstrate social enterprise.

The Converging World (TCW) invites donations from individuals and businesses so that it may build renewable energy installations in developing countries. It then applies the income streams from electricity in those countries to projects for sustainable livelihoods, while the income streams from carbon credits are directed at creating low-carbon lifestyles in developed nations.

This is the story of how The Converging World grew from local actions in a village in the UK to become an international charity. However, we shall also look closely at the larger picture, particularly the development of local, community-led sustainability groups and their future development. By proposing the concept of convergence as the driving force for action and reflection, we offer a framework to evaluate how communities and projects may develop to meet the challenges and opportunities we face.

The beginning

It all began with the Royal Society of Arts, Commerce and Manufacture (usually known as the RSA), which celebrated its 250th anniversary in March 2004 by starting the Coffeehouse Challenges; this was a return to its origins in the coffee shops of eighteenth-century London. The 'challenges' were a simple idea to get people talking about big issues, with the hope that their conversations would generate action. The RSA programme considered five challenges to shape our society:

- Encouraging Enterprise
- Moving Towards a Zero-Waste Society
- Fostering Resilient Communities
- Developing a Capable Population
- Advancing Global Citizenship

In Bristol, a medium-sized city in the south-west of the UK, the local branch of the RSA picked up the challenge of 'Moving Towards a Zero-Waste Society', and a series of meetings were held over coffee in Starbucks cafés.

At roughly the same time, the villagers of Chew Magna, eight miles south of the city, were collating the results of a survey for a parish plan. Everyone had been asked for their opinions on all aspects of the environment and social organisation and how they would like to see their community develop. The outcome of this consultation was a glossy report and an exhibition in the village hall. One of the visitors to the exhibition was involved in the Bristol RSA process, and he made a connection: why not try for a zero-waste village? It was a startling idea – it was as if the parish plan came from a 'business as usual' worldview, while zero waste was a completely different perspective: one that accepted the need for fundamental shifts in thinking. It wasn't long before the RSA influence took hold, and a few people had organised a series of coffeehouse conversations in the village – with no preconceptions as to any outcome or actions. After these initial chats over coffee, several more gatherings happened – a few in the pub for those not around in the daytime. Each time the discussion was lively and the numbers swelled.

This first response was surprising – something had tapped deeply into the consciousness of the local population and had released energy. Not only were people concerned, even anxious, but it was apparent that they were keen to make something happen. When, one evening, more than forty people turned up, it was too late to stop the momentum and soon four groups formed to take action.

Three of the groups were obvious clusters of interest. The Energy and Transport group had ideas ranging from simply improving energy efficiency like loft insulation advice through to ambitious schemes for microhydro generation using the local river. The Waste and Recycling group formed to tackle the output streams – the rubbish, the physical, visible waste – while the People and Consumption group dealt with lifestyles and input streams: goods, packaging, food and other supplies.

The fourth group was slightly different: outward- rather than inward-looking, it emerged as people responded to a global rather than a local dialogue. It was made up of people thinking about global problems and how local actions affect, indirectly, the lives of others far away. One immediate, and again obvious, concern was sustainable travel: how much we travel and what we do when we are abroad. Another concern was about social justice, fair trade and the production of the goods and services that we import, along with the extended supply chains of which we have little knowledge. The people particularly interested in these global issues held coffeehouse conversations and formed into what they called the Converging World group.

The idea takes off, and Go Zero is formed

The four groups developed quickly and created an urgency to do something. However, there was a need to discover the extent of the concern in the community as a whole. Were those who had so far registered their interest the only ones, or were there many more who would like to get involved? An Open Day was organised, with each group assigned a corner of the village hall to display ideas and to host discussions. The children had a special area in the middle for making useful things from waste.

A glossy, four-sided newsletter was delivered to every house in the area. This presented the ideas, and it invited people to come along and to lend their support. The day exceeded expectations by far: it was buzzing as if the event had released the desire to talk about these issues with a view to doing something about them. What also appeared was a great deal of knowledge, skill and experience that was held, almost invisibly, in a community like this. As a result of that day 150 people signed up, and there was a name and a logo for the future: Go Zero.

The enthusiasm was picked up and magnified by the media: the local press gave full descriptions, and the regional press followed. The Go Zero story was pertinent and timely for the beginning of the frenzy of articles about climate change and environmental problems that is still raging today. The national press followed: two daily newspapers had full page spreads, and the film crews moved in, culminating with Chew Magna as a feature on the BBC news. A lot of noise about not very much, but it was what people wanted to hear. The message was clear: you could do something, however small, which mattered.

Three to four years later, and the work in the village continues with more projects, newsletters, open days, surveys and meetings. Go Zero has a range of activities aimed at awareness, monitoring, education and demonstration. In its small way it has stimulated and inspired other communities, but it is now in for the long haul – twenty years at least.

Although the general awareness of global issues, especially climate change, has increased greatly since Go Zero started, projects like this have to face a constituency that have seen their wealth increase and, until recently, the price of the fuel for their cars remain stable. There are concerns, but they are just dark clouds on the horizon, rather than having any immediate impact on daily life – it's all in the future or far away. Have initiatives like Go Zero run out? Have they reached their limit in the current economic climate? Will groups like this come into their own when times get difficult, or will people abandon them as they retreat into self-preservation?

How did The Converging World emerge?

Early on in Go Zero's life, the Converging World group formed links with an organisation in Tamil Nadu in southern India called Social Change and Development (SCAD). However, some people in Go Zero were sensitive to the possibilities that this link might detract from the efforts to support the existing community links in the village, especially if we were trying to raise funds for SCAD.

The media exposure meant that other communities started to form, and it was natural for some protagonists in the group to see thousands of

Go Zeros across the country. A dilemma arose. Go Zero was, and is, a village project focused in a specific locality, yet there was an ambition among some to spread it, to connect to other communities, to organise and develop a network.

Two threads were emerging, leading to The Converging World (TCW). One was the desire to link communities across the continents. The other was a vision of spreading the idea of community action and forming connections among the groups that were springing up in the UK. Neither of these threads is straightforward.

A third thread in the development of TCW arrived with Go Zero's Carbon Club. This was a local scheme formed to allow members to offset their carbon emissions.

An evening meeting about climate change and offsetting presented the idea that you could pay to get trees planted to absorb the approximately ten tonnes of carbon dioxide emissions for which each person was responsible annually. This idea went down like the proverbial lead balloon. Go Zeroites were not that naïve. They had gathered into a concerned group to do things. They were not interested in a scheme that asked them to pay up to something unseen, wash their hands and carry on as before, however worthy the projects were on which the money would be spent.

This mismatch of visions was keenly debated. There was a kernel of something important in offsetting, it provided an accumulation of money which enabled action, but the feeling was that it had to be linked to carbon reduction in the here and now; it needed to work for changes within our own lives.

What emerged was the idea to start a community carbon-offset scheme. To keep it simple, Go Zero created a carbon club and invited members to donate on a self-assessed basis. By collecting this money directly it was under Go Zero's control, as long as it was within the stated objectives of the constitution:

> The club will apply all monies raised to schemes that aim to reduce greenhouse gas emissions or otherwise mitigate the effects of climate change, or counteract environmental and social degradation.

This third thread – a locally controlled, carbon-offsetting scheme – was one more component in the tapestry leading to The Converging World.

It was considered important to understand what kind of support the people in Tamil Nadu might need from the people of Chew Magna, to identify the role which each community would play in this partnership and to find out how an exchange of ideas and initiatives would generate win-win outcomes. Luckily, visits from India to Chew Magna allowed personal relationships to form. Subsequent visits to India built on this, and ideas for connection arose. Somehow the idea formed to provide a wind turbine in India. It was a challenge that might have seemed impossible at first, but it stuck, and it seemed to fit well with carbon offsetting.

This idea emerged to meet the growing demand in India for electricity by supplying renewable energy that substitutes for fossil-fuel-generated power. The carbon emissions saved in this way (in the form of carbon credits) are increasingly valuable to businesses and individuals in the UK who wish to meet their obligations to reduce but, as yet, can only partly achieve that by changing what they do.

And so a triple win started to appear: one – a reduction in carbon emissions; two – income from selling electricity is channelled to poor communities to achieve sustainable livelihoods; and three – donations, in exchange for saved carbon emissions, are used to fund projects and campaigns to contract consumption in the rich communities of the demanding world.

Of course, this would also bring added benefits. We will achieve even bigger wins than these three put together by forging links between communities, by changing hearts and minds and by generating hope through action.

'An elegant strategy'

After many discussions and many thoughtful hours, The Converging World emerged. Its immediate aims are simple, and follow three steps.

The first step is to raise donations from individuals and businesses anywhere in the world so that it can install renewable energy facilities like 1.5 megawatt wind turbines in Tamil Nadu, southern India. These installations will save carbon emissions that would otherwise be created by burning coal; 60% of India's electric power is generated from coal.

The second step is to sell the electricity generated by the wind turbine onto the Indian national grid. Some of this income is used to pay off loans to buy more turbines to multiply – and so leverage – the effect, and The Converging World is committing 25% of the net proceeds to SCAD, who have worked tirelessly for sustainable livelihoods in this region for more than twenty years. However, there is a great need for more money to bring thousands of people out of desperate poverty. This commitment is to sustainable economic development.

Meanwhile, the third step is back in the developed world, in the UK initially. The wind turbines are destined to be accredited under the Clean Development Mechanism of the UN Framework Convention on Climate Change (UNFCCC). They will also meet the Gold Standard for carbon credits that sets criteria for the social and environmental impact that the project makes in the country. The wind turbines create a stream of carbon credits that have a value, either for those companies or organisations which are obliged to purchase them or for those who wish to demonstrate their commitment to the carbon emission agenda. The Converging World will convert the credits into money which is then applied to projects which seek carbon reduction.

On more than one occasion, the concept that The Converging World has created has been called an elegant strategy, and Aubrey Meyer, the originator of the Contraction and Convergence concept,[1] has described it as "a beautiful model". It is known by some as a triple-decker sandwich approach because of its three distinct benefits.

The Converging World is based on, and goes beyond, the principles of Contraction and Convergence. It proposes that we reduce consumption of resources, energy and the emission of greenhouse gases in the demanding world while accepting an increasing consumption in developing and deprived sectors. It is a vision to which all communities can strive towards – each of us using an equal share that, in total, the Earth can bear. But convergence means much more than seeking worldwide convergence of resource use and wealth and extends to the following:

- Convergence is a complex concept involving carbon emissions, climate change and energy, cultural diversity, differing values, technological change, human rights, spiritual challenges, political power, social struggles and resistance. All these dimensions interact as increases in population and consumption are stretching the planet's capacity beyond its limits.

- Convergence means reducing the ecological footprint of some while increasing that of others. This is a difficult idea for those of us with a high-demand lifestyle; it implies shrinking our consumption so that others may expand theirs, and shrinking to such an extent that the total impact is bearable by the ecological, economic and social systems we inhabit. This is a tough target physically and spiritually, but we must meet it while not blaming anyone for the predicament we are in.

- Convergence means resistance and struggle to obtain equal access to health, education and welfare. It would be wonderful if actions to reach these goals came from the top through international agreements. However, this occurs half-heartedly because of the system's need to stay focused on opinion polls. Grassroots momentum is therefore vital, although it is likely to be a long road which will need patience, acceptance and persistence.

- Convergence means creating a just society where people can live freely, fearlessly, and receive a fair reward for their contribution to their community. We must seek methods to transcend or reduce the barriers to freedom, whether social, economic, political, philosophical and psychological which prevent this equality.

There is nothing startlingly new in any of these ideas. What we present, however, is a practical way to combine them to allow much more to be created than is put in. We have a process of persuade, use, use, use, and then persuade again:

1. Persuade everyone in the demanding world that they should donate money in recognition of their carbon impact and the fact that we are facing an extremely worrying future.
2. Use the donations to build renewable energy installations in the developing world.
3. Use the proceeds of sale of the electricity to drive sustainable economic development for the poorest people on the planet.
4. Use the carbon-credit income for contraction in the demanding world, through efficiency, renewable technologies and social change. This reduces energy demand and carbon emissions.
5. Persuade people that what they thought was a problem is really a massive opportunity to reshape their lives with greater meaning, quality and happiness.

The Converging World is an established charity. It has met all the criticisms of carbon offsetting and is now promoting the opportunities which emerge from necessarily complex solutions to complex problems.

The Consortium Fund concept

The Converging World invites individuals, businesses and other organisation to join and to make donations which go beyond carbon neutral by not only recognising and reflecting on their CO_2 emissions and consequently their impact on the planet but also by supporting sustainable community development. To achieve its multiple objectives it uses the mechanism of renewable energy and its two income streams – electricity income and carbon credits – to provide a 'funding engine'.

The Converging World has created the concept of a consortium fund to enable communities to own the idea and in many ways to make it local. A consortium is a community or group of individuals or organisations which have something in common. The obvious communities are those defined by geography – a village, a town or part of a city – but there are many other types of community, such as professional associations, sports clubs and their supporters, special interest groups, groups of concerned employees, schools and trade associations.

Any group may form a Converging World consortium fund to hold the donations for its community. When the fund reaches a certain level the community acquires a share of a wind turbine in increments of 1% of a turbine at a time. When this happens, The Converging World will start a proportionate flow of carbon credit income to whichever organisation the community chooses: this could be itself, to support its objectives, or another organisation with social and/or environmental goals. Putting this in terms of numbers, a 1% share of a turbine requires that £12,500 be raised by a community. This triggers the payment of £1,000 a year, indefinitely, back to that community for carbon reduction work. At the same time there is a flow of electricity income in India for sustainable economic development.

The consortium fund idea is designed to generate ownership, creativity and participation whilst providing a practical focus for carbon reduction efforts.

Sustainable communities

And so we return to the valley. Another cycle of action begins with a consortium fund called Target 60 (the UK government has set a target of 60% reduction in emissions by 2050). The residents and the businesses in the whole of the Chew Valley of around 15,000 households south of Bristol will be invited to join. Maybe only 3-4% will do so, but that is enough to start, enough to contribute to the TCW model and produce a flow of income to support the dedicated few who will keep on working to change the way we live and start community-scale actions in this valley. What else can we do? Target 60 is a long-term project. If the concept of donating takes hold in this community, then TCW offers a steadily increasing source of money to enable community-scale activity, owned by the people, as Target 60 is a Community Interest Company, doing what individuals alone cannot achieve.

What can we learn about communities from Go Zero and The Converging World? It is salutary to reflect on what we are trying to do and to learn from the experiences of being part of a group that has gone through some remarkable times. The Go Zero mantra seems increasingly pertinent: 'No Blame, Can Do and Patience'. Looking at what is happening, at the processes, we can divide them into three phases, elements of which can go forward concurrently and they demonstrate an unfolding of awareness of the issues, see Table 1.1 (opposite).

Phase I is all about self, about first-person, singular actions that follow on from first-person reflection about one's place in the scheme of events and one's responsibilities. It seems like the mundane: turn off the standby on the TV, change to low-energy light bulbs, save water, and eschew the use of plastic bags and so on. Little things, irrelevant in their impact as individual actions, even if magnified seem barely more than a pinprick in the problem. However, as a means to channel a sense of hopelessness towards meaning, they are essential as first steps. It is a personal transformation.

Phase II is first person plural action: it is about us as a community taking action together. This is where larger-scale and bigger-impact changes can occur. It opens up the possibility of schemes like micro-generation, new forms of waste collection, car clubs, skills-swapping and local currencies – anything that requires co-operation and sharing. This intra-community action is done for the benefit of those within the group. It should lead to improved social cohesion and can be described as building resilience, which is the ability to withstand external shocks and to adapt to changes from outside. It has a focus on the internal infrastructure of the community, both physical processes like energy, waste streams and transport, and the social relationships that produce increased sharing and care for one another.

	Examples of action	Focus	Awareness	Processes
Phase I **Individual** **Lifestyle**	Light bulbs, energy efficiency in the home, waste separation, saving water. An end to plastic bags, home composting, loft insulation, less travel by car, use of bikes and buses. Household cost savings.	Behavioural (me)	Self-centred actions that contribute to the general good	Personal consumption and disposal
Phase II **Intra-community** **Communal action**	Local currencies, lift-sharing, car clubs, community micro-generation. Waste collection services, fund-raising for own projects. Biofuels from waste, aggregated buying, local food, skill-swapping.	Resilience (us)	Inward-looking, improving the survival chances of the group. Building local relationships	Providing for the local community infrastructure
Phase III **Inter-community** **Global conscience**	Fair trade, eco-tourism, community twinning, responsible eco-trade. Offsetting and micro-finance initiatives. Lobbying and democratic pressure for top-down policy change.	Convergence (us and them)	Aware of systemic interdependence and focused on creating and maintaining relationships over distances. Servicing the local through co-operation.	Community linking and integration. Conscience and participatory economics. Political pressure.

Table 1.1: The sustainable community group development table

Phase III is 'us and them': it goes far beyond resilience to consider that no community is isolated and able to become self-sufficient. There is a danger that Phase II thinking becomes fixed on the group, becomes inward-looking and the delusion arises that by improving resilience then we will survive by ourselves – whatever happens out there. Phase III is much more concerned with systems thinking and realising the interdependence of all communities. Although there may be a few residual communities that have no direct connection to any other, indirectly every one is connected through the planet and, especially, we all share the atmosphere. The essential word for Phase III is 'convergence'; that is, the realisation that our communities' ecological impact on the planet should reduce where it is too high and rise where it is too low. It is a drive towards ecological justice coupled with social justice. This is the theoretical concept behind The Converging World and is discussed further by John Pontin and Ian Roderick in a recent Schumacher Briefing.[2]

The Converging World places the emphasis on Phase III thinking. As this century unfolds, and times get tough, we will see severe strains on our relationships across communities and nations. It is often said that most wars are fought over resources, whatever political or religious veneer is used to cover these facts. As oil depletes and we hit periods of shortages of energy and food, as climates change and places become hostile to life, then people will fight or they will move to other areas, already populated, to seek resources as basic as water. The tensions are obvious, the outlook bleak.

TCW's purpose is to raise awareness of these different and difficult futures and to reduce the divergence through greater linking of communities, but more importantly by finding mechanisms for convergence of wealth and the use of resources. These mechanisms are underpinned by the transfer of money – by getting people to understand the need to pay more than the current economic system enables by valuing what in reality creates quality of life but which is taken for granted and, consequently, undervalued or invisible: effectively it's about valuing nature, human relationship and human justice. The work of TCW, therefore, is about 'conscience economics', which goes beyond choosing fair-trade goods that reward producers better; for donating and offsetting are powerful ways to say that you care, that you are in the process of change and that you want to contribute now. It is as much, if not more, about care of the self as care of the other. In this setting it is important to be clear about what 'care of the self' means. It does not advocate hedonism.

The sustainable community group movement

In the same way that we see three different phases for what happens within sustainable community groups, these three phases are reflected in the way that the community group 'movement' is evolving as can be seen in Table 1.2 (below). The first phase is where many groups operate in relative isolation – there are contacts made between groups, but no close involvement. The experience with Go Zero in particular has been one where many invitations have arrived asking for a speaker to come and talk to a newly formed group in another village, but afterwards only a few email exchanges might occur – little ongoing sharing of experiences.

The second phase is now appearing (in 2008). This is where networks are forming and loose coalitions of groups start to work together. The Transition Towns Initiative has a well-defined process and network for

	Awareness	Focus	Example
Phase I **Individual community groups**	Sense of local community concerns	Isolated, interacting with local authorities on local issues	Go Zero and many others
Phase II **Connected community groups**	Sharing ideas to project a grassroots voice for policy changes	Networking and sharing within one region/ nation. Talking to national government	Transition Initiative Low Carbon Communities Network
Phase III **Global integration of community groups**	Cross-region/nation working with the concept of interdependence	Convergence – deliberate actions to affect other communities. Engaging in global governance	The Converging World?

Table 1.2. The sustainable community group movement development table

sharing through a common development process.[3] The Low Carbon Communities Network is a new coalition that is attempting to present a common voice to government at all levels – representing sustainable community groups *en masse* to replace the previously untargeted approach of individual groups lobbying their own representatives.

The third phase, we believe, has yet to materialise. This phase is the deliberate linking of community groups across the many divides and divergences that exist in this world; linking with the objective of reducing those destructive and divisive differences, i.e. deliberate attempts at convergence.

Will this phase emerge? It is probably the most important thing that could emerge from the reaction to the dire prognostications about the future. Yet emergent properties are ephemeral, they are not certain. The negative pulls of scepticism and cynicism, especially from within, are always stifling. Those most involved are those who can kill what they love.

Conclusion

The authors of this chapter are researchers and come from the schools of critical theory, systems thinking and action research. The nature of this research is not objective study from a distance; it is the opposite. It is getting stuck in, hands dirty, attending many evening meetings in draughty village halls and being an integral part of the action. It is aimed at improving lives, working with a vision of a future that is far larger than the project's immediate goals.

Building The Converging World is an idealistic endeavour, yet two large turbines are currently under construction, with many more on order, and money is flowing into projects in the UK and in India.

Many people's lives have been affected already, and it is often the case that, as Buskens and Earl write, "Emancipatory action researchers know that their calling demands that they be deeply involved in the process, and furthermore that they themselves will likely change as a result."[4] This is the case here: we would like to acknowledge the vision of others, their enquiries into the meaning of this work, their efforts to overcome difficulties, to adapt and to learn, above all their dedication to making The Converging World happen.

* * *

References
I. Buskens and S. Earl (2008) 'Outcome Mapping and Emancipatory Action Research', *Action Research*, Vol. 6 No. 2.

R. Hopkins (2008) *The Transition Handbook: from oil dependency to local resilience*, Green Books.

A. Meyer (2000) *Contraction and Convergence: The Global Solution to Climate Change* (Schumacher Briefing No. 5), Green Books.

J. Pontin and I. Roderick (2007) *Converging World: Connecting Communities in Global Change* (Schumacher Briefing No. 13), Green Books.

Notes
1. See Meyer 2000 for further information on 'contraction and convergence'. This is one of a number of sustainability briefings produced by the Schumacher Society.

2. See Pontin and Roderick 2007.

3. See Hopkins 2008.

4. Buskens and Earl 2008.

Chapter Two

NGOs: The *sine qua non* of adapting to climate change in Africa

by Siobhan Riordan MA

Sine qua non, originally a Latin legal term, means 'without which it could not be' ('but for'). It refers to an indispensable and essential action, condition or ingredient.

Global warming is now leading to changes in climate that have potentially devastating consequences for the peoples of Africa. Climate exerts significant control on the day-to-day economic development of Africa, particularly for the agricultural and water-resources sectors, at regional, local and household scales. This chapter brings together postgraduate research[1] to examine strategies organisations need to consider when addressing climate change in Africa. From this research a compelling case emerges that suggests non-governmental organisations (NGOs) in particular are essential and indispensable actors to cultivate adaptation to climate change in rural villages.

In the last three decades, NGOs have proliferated in number and become increasingly influential players in global politics. This proliferation has been driven by grassroots mobilisation amongst poor communities as well as top-down approaches to development. The 1980s and 1990s saw the rise of what has been described as a pro-NGO norm among donor states and intergovernmental organisations (IGOs) such as the United Nations, which has actively promoted the spread of NGOs to developing countries.[2] By the 1990s, there were an estimated 250,000 NGOs operating at the grassroots level in Asia, Africa and Latin America alone.[3] Many of these NGOs are found in the communities that are home to some of the most vulnerable populations to climate change in the world.

It is now widely accepted that the increase of greenhouse gases in the climate is due to human activities. The enhanced greenhouse effect is likely to be large enough to have an impact on global and regional climates. According to the UN's Intergovernmental Panel on Climate Change (IPCC) 4th assessment of scientific knowledge, the atmospheric concentrations of CO_2 (a greenhouse gas) in 2005 exceed by far the natural range over the last 650,000 years. Global increases in CO_2 concentrations are due primarily to fossil fuel use, with land-use change providing another significant but smaller contribution.

Because climate change is linked to human activities, it means we have the power to do something about it. After all, as an old Peruvian proverb says:

> We have not inherited the Earth from our parents, we are borrowing it from our children.

If we are to protect that which is entrusted to us, then action to tackle climate change is vital. Although climate change is a global issue, much of the action is required at the local level, and the precise nature of interventions depends on local circumstances. This chapter begins with a brief analysis of climate change vulnerability, impact and adaptive capacity in Africa, set within a context of inequality and injustice. It draws attention to the essential role of grassroots organising at the local level, if vulnerable communities are to adapt to climate change. It explores adaptation through a sustainable-development lens, and assesses the significance of NGOs in leading adaptation in Africa. It examines strategies for community-based adaptation and highlights the importance of women's leadership and participation. It looks at ways in which communities are exploiting opportunities from climate change. The conclusion brings together this analysis to suggest a compelling case for making NGO development a critical element for effective and sustainable adaptation strategies to climate change.

Unequal impacts

Climate change is now a growing reality for all peoples across the world. The impact of climate change however, is not so equal. According to the IPCC, Africa is one of the regions most vulnerable to the impacts of climate change and its precursor of climate variability. 70% of the peoples of Africa live in rural areas. Poverty has led to economic migration, with men leaving to work in urban areas to earn a family income. This has left many female-headed households in rural villages. Among the risks the continent faces are reductions in food security and agricultural productivity, particularly regarding subsistence agriculture, increased water stress and, as a result of these, the potential for increased exposure to disease and other health risks.[4] IPCC Climate Change Scenarios of the future suggest that:

- By 2020, 75-250 million people are projected to be exposed to increased water stress.
- By 2020, yields from rain-fed agriculture could be reduced by 50%.
- By 2080, an increase of arid and semi-arid land in Africa.

In other words, in just twelve years time millions of people will be faced with impacts from climate change that have potentially devastating consequences for rural livelihoods in Africa.

According to the IPCC, the science of climate change scenarios concludes that Africa is already experiencing climate variability and is expected to get hotter and drier in the future. Long-term temperatures are increasing, with pronounced changes in the timing of rains and frequency of droughts. This has led to an increase in the associated hazards of drought, flood, deforestation, disease and natural disasters. This shift in temperature and precipitation is already having and will continue to have a severe impact on agriculture, water supply, land use, livestock and human health in Africa. Tackling these changes is critical for those most vulnerable to the impacts of global warming.

There are two kinds of strategy for dealing with climate change. A mitigation strategy focuses on practices or policies to reduce greenhouse gas emissions. An adaptation strategy increases capacity to cope with, and exploit, the opportunities of climate change. Mitigation strategies are generally at the state, national, and international levels. Adaptation strategies are generally aimed at the local level. Most strategies to tackle climate change to date have focused largely on mitigation strategies. It is only recently that adaptation strategies have begun to receive attention. The localised nature of adaptation makes it of particular relevance for Africa, because the majority of people live in rural villages. Protecting these rural populations from climate change impacts requires a village-level approach. An organisation wishing to develop a policy for adaptation to future climate change might best begin by assessing current vulnerability to the present-day climate, including its variability and extremes.[5]

Climate change vulnerability

Vulnerability to climate change is classified as: exposure to changes in the climate; sensitivity – the degree to which a system is affected by or responsive to climate stimuli; and adaptive capacity – the ability to prepare for, respond to, and tackle the effects of climate change (see Figure 2.1).

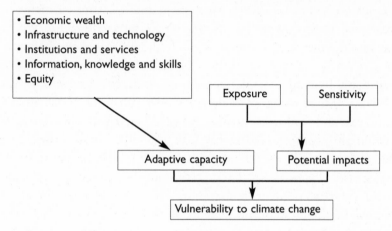

Figure 2.1. Vulnerability to climate change: the IPCC Third Assessment Report

Africa scores poorly on all three criteria. The geography of Africa leaves it particularly exposed. Being such a large land mass means that interior countries especially will suffer greater increases in temperature than the average warming elsewhere. Populations in Africa are particularly sensitive to the direct impacts of climate change because of their heavy dependency on rain-fed agriculture and ecosystems that are already degraded in many parts. It is estimated that 70% of Africa's population are currently dependent on subsistence (daily survival through rain-fed food and fuel production for the family household) agriculture. Rapid and future population growth, widespread poverty, food insecurity and ill health increase sensitivity. People will adapt to changes in the climate as far as their knowledge and resources allow. Across Africa, poor governance, a lack of infrastructure (most notably in the area of water supply and management), poor financial means and access to public services all undermine adaptive capacity.[6]

Sub-Saharan Africa is the most vulnerable region, and home to an estimated 740 million people. Southern Africa, for example, is already experiencing the devastation of climate variability, with four years of drought from 2004 and floods in 2007, destroying livelihoods and creating humanitarian crises across the region. Adaptive capacity is also undermined by HIV/AIDS, with the death of parent generations diminishing industrial and agricultural capabilities, and losing vital indigenous ecological knowledge that should have been passed on to future generations. For example, in Zimbabwe 2,000 people die each week from AIDS, resulting in an average life span of 34 years for women and 37 years for men. An AIDS-weakened society alone has consequences for the social fabric of Africa far into the future, never mind about adding the impacts of climate change.

In their analysis of adaptation research, the 4th IPCC Assessment concluded: "The capacity to adapt is dynamic and influenced by economic and natural resources, social networks, entitlements, institutions and governance, human resources, and technology. Multiple stresses related to HIV/AIDS, land degradation, trends in economic globalisation, and violent conflict affect exposure to climate risks and the capacity to adapt."[7] Widespread poverty, conflict, disease and environmental degradation combine to undermine adaptive capacity in Africa. Combine this with mass dependency on rain-fed agriculture, and it leaves the peoples of rural villages in Africa particularly vulnerable to climate variability and change.

And amongst these people, there is one particular group that is exposed to multiple vulnerabilities: women. One of the primary reasons that women are more vulnerable to the effects of climate change is that they are disproportionately dependent on threatened natural resources. Women are responsible for approximately 75% of household food production in sub-Saharan Africa.[8] The IPCC predicts that yields from rain-fed agriculture in sub-Saharan Africa could be reduced by as much as 50% by 2020. The dependency on subsistence agriculture for many poor rural women leaves them particularly exposed to the impacts of climate change.

The wide range of threats and hazards from climate change that are facing Africa are intertwined with gender inequality. Climate change exacerbates existing inequalities and slows progress toward gender equality. Gender equality is a known prerequisite for sustainable development and

Threats due to climate change	Gender implications
• Reduction of agricultural production for survival and commercial ends • Food security at risk • Less access to safe water	• Loss of domestic species of plants and animals used by women to ensure food security of their families • Reduction, mobilisation, or extinction of marine species used by women for household consumption for productive activities • Increase in women's workload due to decline in availability of water and other resources.
• Increase in the workload needed for agricultural production and subsistence activities • Environmental changes are likely to drive migration	• Generally, girls and women are responsible for the collection of water and firewood. If the time they invest in these tasks increases, their capacity to attend school is at risk • According to UNHCR, 80% of refugees in the world are women and children. Migration of populations, given extreme changes and disasters, could interrupt and limit the opportunities for education • Men are more likely to migrate, either seasonally or for a number of years. Female-headed households left behind are often the poorest. The workloads of these women, their children and the elderly increase significantly as a result of male emigration.
• Environmental effects can aggravate the risk of contracting serous illnesses • Increased prevalence of some vector-borne diseases • Increase in temperatures	• Increase in women's workload due to their role as primary carers in the family • Loss of medicinal plants used by women • Pregnant women are particularly susceptible to water-borne diseases. Anaemia – resulting from malaria – is responsible for a quarter of maternal mortalities • Women and children are fourteen times more likely to die than men during a disaster • The high mortality rates of mothers/women/spouses during disasters result in an increase in: the number of orphans and mortality rates; early marriages for young girls, causing them to drop out of school; trafficking and prostitution which in turn increases exposure to HIV/AIDS • Migration enhances the risk of getting HIV/AIDS, given that families are separated and they are forced to live in overpopulated spaces • In developing countries, the poorer households affected by HIV/AIDS have less resources to adapt to the impacts of climate change. The need to adopt new strategies for crop production (such as irrigation) or mobilisation of livestock is harder for female-headed households and for houses with HIV-infected people.
• Extinction of species, changes in species composition, disruption of symbiotic relationships, changes in trophic cascades, among others • Changes in the quantity and quality of natural resources could reduce the productivity of ecosystems • Floods, droughts, rising sea levels, melting of glaciers and polar icecaps	• Without secure access to and control over natural resources (land, water, livestock, trees) women are less likely to be able to cope with climate change impacts • Less available drinking water means women have to expend more effort to collect, store, protect and distribute water • Adaptation measures, related to anti-desertification, are often labour-intensive and women face increasing expectations to contribute unpaid household and community labour to soil and water conservations efforts • Decrease in forest resources used by women • Women often rely on a range of crop varieties to accommodate climate variability, but permanent temperature change will reduce agro-biodiversity and traditional medicine options • Lack of representatives and women's participation in the decision-making spheres related to climate change at all levels (local, national and international).

Table 2.1: Gendered Impacts of Climate Change (adapted from Aguilar, 2007)

poverty reduction. The inequalities that are magnified by climate change slow down progress toward these development goals as well. In a similar manner, gender inequality worsens the impacts of climate change.[9] Table 2.1 describes a range of threats from climate change and highlights the different vulnerabilities for women. It provides a compelling case for why women must be integral when assessing vulnerability to climate change.

Inequalities are compounded by the gender blindness of development programmes. For example, FAO1 studies demonstrate that whilst women in most developing countries are the mainstay of agricultural sectors, the farm labour force and food systems, they have been the last to benefit from – or in some cases have been negatively affected by – prevailing economic growth and development processes. Gender bias and gender blindness persist: farmers are still generally perceived as 'male' by policy-makers, development planners and agricultural service deliverers. For this reason, women find it more difficult than men to gain access to valuable resources such as land, credit and agricultural inputs, technology, extension, training and services that would enhance their productive capacity.[10] In addition to their dependency on agriculture, women's vulnerability is increased by the blindness of development initiatives to their leadership and participation in food production and household livelihood.

As crop yields decline and resources become scarcer, women's workloads will expand. In times of drought, they will also have to spend more time performing another typical female responsibility – carrying, purifying and supplying the family's water. According to one study, fetching water for domestic consumption in a Zimbabwean family showed that women contributed 91% to this task, with men spending 1 hour per week on this chore and women 9.3 hours.[11] Moreover, as water- and heat-related diseases increase because of climate change, women will bear the extra burdens of increased care-giving and increased threats to their own health.[12] This additional double burden compounds vulnerability for women in Africa.

Tackling climate change

When looking at the options for tackling climate change, the compounded nature of vulnerabilities led the IPCC to conclude that "the covariant mix of climate stresses and other factors in Africa means that for many in

Africa adaptation is not an option but a necessity."[13] Adaptation is about addressing exposure, reducing a person or system's sensitivity to risk and increasing the resilience or coping capacity.

Several recent climate change impact-modelling studies have shown the importance of adaptation measures in "substantially decreasing potentially adverse impacts of climate change and in strengthening the benefits associated with changes in climate".[14] Investing in adaptation measures can help villages build resilience and shift from vulnerability to strength in the face of climate change. Cultivating this adaptation is a key strategy for organisations supporting villages in Africa.

Much of the investment available for adaptation focuses on techno-engineering responses to the physical impacts of climate change. These fail to take into account the socio-economic dynamics that shape the vulnerability to climate change that is particularly evident in Africa. In recent years, there has been a recognition that adaptation measures cannot focus solely on the physical impacts of climate change. They also need to address the underlying socio-economic, institutional, political and cultural factors, that determine how people respond to, and cope with, climate hazards.[15] Adaptation initiatives can therefore include livelihood enhancement, poverty alleviation, education, improved institutional arrangements, and strengthening food security. These activities generally fall under sustainable development. Adaptation strategies therefore need to focus on integrating climate change into sustainable development initiatives.[16] A sustainable development approach to climate change will help to address the multiple vulnerabilities that currently undermine adaptive capacity in Africa.

International responsibility

Any examination of the relationship between climate change and Africa inevitably leads to confrontation with a final injustice to stir consciences. Whilst Africa remains one of the most vulnerable regions to climate change, they have contributed least to greenhouse gas emissions. As Figure 2.2 shows, Africa represents only a small fraction – 3.6% – of the total carbon dioxide (CO_2) emissions per year:[17]

Climate change impacts are set to intensify, yet the poorest communities are unable to cope with current climatic (and other) shocks, let alone any future risks related to climate change. It is vital that these communities are helped to adapt to climate change. Exposure, sensitivity, low adaptive capacity, poor governance and injustice mean that international support is critical to cultivate adaptation in Africa. And it is those responsible for escalating greenhouse gas emissions – the polluters – that need to pay. And that means people from rich countries. Oxfam estimates that adapting to climate change in developing countries is likely to cost at least $50bn each year, and far more if global greenhouse gas emissions are not

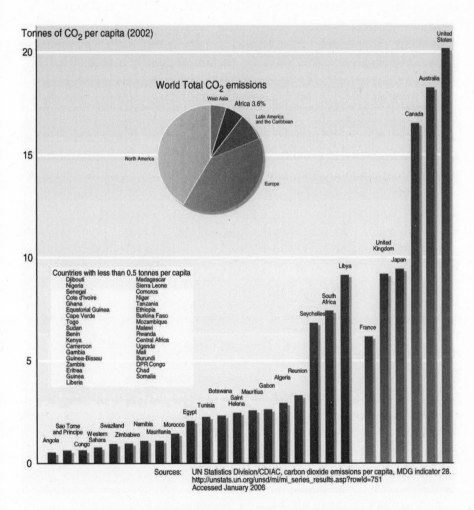

Figure 2.2: Emissions of carbon dioxide in Africa and selected OECD countries.
*Source: http://maps.grida.no/go/graphic/emissions_of_carbon_dioxide_*
in_africa_and_selected_oecd_countries

cut fast enough. Yet so far international donors have increased their contributions to overseas development assistance (ODA) by a mere $43m for urgent adaptation needs.[18] And past experience has clearly shown that simply providing governments of poor countries with aid does not mean that it will reach the poor and most vulnerable.[19]

Those most vulnerable to climate change in Africa largely come from marginalised, remote areas and receive limited services or support from their governments. Reaching the hundreds of millions of people in them will be an immense challenge for any international or national funding mechanisms.

Helping the millions of people at greatest risk from climate change to adapt to its impacts, seems a daunting task. Tackling climate change hazards in Africa means addressing multiple vulnerabilities. "The reverse of vulnerability is capacity, which can be described as the resources of individuals, households, communities, institutions and nations to resist the impact of a hazard." [20] By focusing on the capabilities of the poor rather than their vulnerability, it provides a starting point for sustainable development that can moderate the negative effects of climate change on agricultural production and empower communities to exploit opportunities. Therefore adaptation strategies in Africa need to focus on creating opportunities that can increase capacity, knowledge and resources for villages to adapt to the changing environment. In recent decades, one group of organisations has proved particularly successful at building capacity in local communities, and these are NGOs.

Sustainable development

By its very nature, adaptation happens at the grassroots level and requires locally sensitive solutions. For those that live in urban or rural areas, to those upstream and those downstream, adaptation solutions will be different and localised. Given the lack of commitment to date from ODA and the already increasing demands on this pool of resources, it implies a need to enhance self-sufficiency. And this is where NGOs have a significant role to play. They have a long-established track record in sustainable development and grassroots empowerment. In developing countries, NGOs are broadly defined as "those organisations engaged in development",[21] and recent decades have seen significant growth in their numbers.

Probably the most comprehensive study of this phenomenon has been undertaken by Julie Fisher (1998). Distinguishing between what she defines as Grass Roots Organisations (GROs) and Grass Roots Support Organisations (GRSOs), she found that there were over 200,000 GROs and 50,000 GRSOs in Africa, Asia, and Latin America. In the last decade this number has grown significantly. GROs are defined as locally-based membership organisations that work to develop their own communities. The proliferation of GRSOs began in the 1960s, with an estimated 50,000 GRSOs active by the 1990s and evidence of a continued increase in these numbers. Although many GROs have been promoted and stimulated by GRSOs, they have also become more active on their own, building networks between GROs and providing a bottom-up stimulus for the proliferation in numbers.

This growth of GROs has been driven by increased availability of official and voluntary foreign assistance. The same decades also saw a dramatic increase in foreign donors providing international NGOs (INGOs) with resources to channel into developing countries. INGOs have also grown in number from 14,000 in 1985, to 21,000 in 2003, to 44,000 in 2008.[22] In parallel, there was widespread investment in universities in developing countries during the 1960s, which produced thousands of professionals with the capacity to create organisations and mobilise grassroots networks. These top-down driving forces have led to hundreds of thousands of GRSOs that are concerned with development, environment, the role of women and primary health care, working in partnership with GROs to create bottom-up driving forces (see Figure 2.3 on next page).

There are some who have come to argue that top-down driving forces have rendered NGOs as mere tools of neoliberalism,[23] being compromised and co-opted in a way that furthers capitalist markets, maintaining poverty, inequality and marginalisation.[24] Others call into question their legitimacy and accountability, arguing that large-scale growth in NGOs has had little development impact, as one commentator concludes: "Western NGOs' desire to help Africans has led them into unhealthy relationships with host countries, donor governments, and media. The result is that they share responsibility for Africa's development disasters."[25] Others argue that the most enthusiastic promoters of NGOs have been Western donor states and IGO officials "committed to universal values promoted by the West". Non-Western states, in contrast, have tended to be far more sceptical of NGOs and have often viewed the rise of NGOs in their own nations as a phenomenon promoted from 'above', by wealthy countries and IGOs.[26]

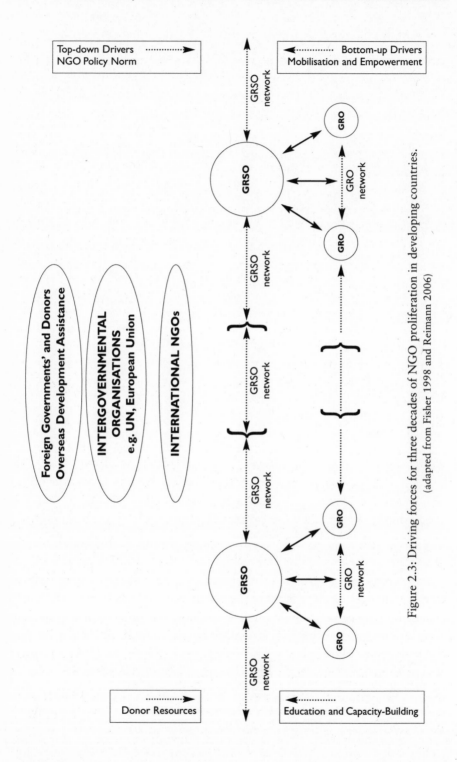

Figure 2.3: Driving forces for three decades of NGO proliferation in developing countries. (adapted from Fisher 1998 and Reimann 2006)

Whilst these criticisms have much validity for Africa, there is a sufficient body of evidence to show that NGOs have made significant contributions to grassroots development and have an unprecedented ability to network across areas and interest groups. As Julie Fisher argues, although many GROs face frustration and failure, there is an immense field-based body of evidence that "GROs are the *sine qua non* of sustainable development".[27] The problem is that this contribution remains largely ignored, especially within climate change literature.

At the grassroots level, experience has shown that GRSOs provide organisational, economic or technological innovations as well as a rapid response to unforeseen opportunities – critical elements for a successful adaptation strategy. GROs, on the other hand, have the potential for a much deeper and more far-reaching impact because they focus on village and household development – the very site for effective adaptation strategies.

Community-based adaptation

Increased resilience to climate stresses can be achieved by enabling communities to enhance their capacity to cope with climate extremes and surprises, such as hurricanes, floods and droughts. In recognition of the localised nature of adaptation and the significance of self-sufficiency, Community-Based Adaptation (CBA) has begun to emerge as an additional (though fairly new) layer of sustainable development activities, practices, research and policies. CBA approaches help to ensure that managing climate change impacts becomes integrated into sustainable development. Although community-based adaptation is an emerging area, NGOs are already leading in the development of participatory methodologies that raise awareness of climate change and foster adaptive capacity.[28]

CBA begins by identifying the communities that are most vulnerable to climate change. Once a community's vulnerability has been established, using the science on climate change impacts, the process of engagement with communities begins. Community-based adaptation recognises that environmental knowledge, vulnerability and resilience to climate impacts are embedded in local cultures. Indigenous knowledge holds many adaptation solutions. This means the focus of CBA is on empowering communities to take action themselves, based on their own decision-making processes.

CBA is a very recent development. NGOs are starting to test CBA activities around the world, and a number of early lessons have already been learned.[29] They include:

- Gain the trust of communities
- Ensure communication on climate change is in the community's own language and uses media such as art, theatre or video rather than the written word
- Identify adaptation strategies that use indigenous capacities, knowledge and practices of coping with climate change
- Set up strategies that factor in climate risk to development activities
- Learning comes from practice itself – adaptation is a classic case of learn-by-doing or action research
- The theory and practice of CBA are in their infancy, therefore as many pilot activities as possible should be carried out to share experience and knowledge.

A CBA approach to managing climate change impacts helps to cultivate indigenous knowledge and improve self-sufficiency through local participation and ownership of development initiatives.

Adaptation strategies

There is a long record of practices to adapt to the impacts of weather as well as natural climate. In terms of dealing with the physical impacts of climate change, agricultural adaptation is a regular feature. In a study of farmers in southern Africa, they found that crop diversification, different planting dates, different varieties, increased varieties, increased use of irrigation, increased use of water and soil conservation techniques are some of the common adaptation options being used by farmers.

Rainwater harvesting is another adaptation strategy that is being successfully used in Zimbabwe to help villages adapt to reduced precipitation and risks of drought. Another study has shown that farms with irrigation are more resistant to changes in climate, indicating that irrigation is also an important adaptation option. An assessment of the economic impacts of climate change on agriculture in southern Africa found that improved education of farmers would do most to hasten adaptation. Similarly, enhanced access to credit, information (climatic and agronomic) as well as to markets (input and output) can significantly increase farm-level adaptation.[30]

Another significant adaptation strategy is to focus on women. According to the IPCC 4th Assessment, "the role of gender in influencing adaptive capacity and adaptation is an important consideration for the development of interventions to enhance adaptive capacity and to facilitate adaptation". Most rural women's greater dependence on the local environmental base for items of daily use increases their stake in the sustainability of that resource base, even though "they cannot be seen as intrinsically more conservationist than men".[31]

Targeting women not only benefits a group significantly affected by climate change. Development literature over the last three decades has consistently shown that women are powerful change agents in a community.[32] Their leadership in community revitalisation and natural resource management is now well established, although often ignored. Perhaps the significance of women's leadership and participation is best understood by looking at what happens when women are ignored.

What happens when gender is ignored?

The absence of a gender perspective results in significant opportunities to promote adaptation being missed. Without a gender analysis, it can obscure the gap between having a stake in environmental protection and the capacity to act on it. Some essential differences in the ways in which men and women typically organise environmental action (usually formal among men, informal among women) can be missed. The absence of gender analysis can lead to a failure to identify the constraints that women face and need to overcome for their effective involvement in the formal institutions of local resource management.

For instance, when introducing new varieties of rice in Asia, development workers only consulted with 'village leaders' who were mainly men, to explain how the new crop should be managed, and did not consult with the women. Consequently, much of the rice was wasted as the actual planters were women, and men did not transfer the new knowledge to them. Similarly, in Thailand, forest officials consulted with village men to implement a community forestry project. Men advised that they needed more hardwood trees for commercial purposes. 3,000 hardwood seedlings were provided, but were left to die. Women in this region care for seedlings, and, as the providers for family subsistence they preferred soft-wood species for fuel wood.

When women's participation has been ignored in water resource management, it has lead to project failure because:

- New water or sanitation facilities fall into disuse and/or disrepair if women have not been consulted about siting, technology, etc
- New facilities cannot be sustained financially by women due to lack of consultation about affordability and financing mechanism and/or lack of provision for maintenance and other ongoing costs
- Female-headed households are excluded from benefits because charges have been set too high.

Ignoring gender also undermines the effectiveness of adaptation strategies. For example, seasonal forecasting is being advocated in Zimbabwe as a specific adaptation strategy. Radio is considered to be a preferred medium for disseminating climate forecast information to subsistence farmers. However, gender analysis in one study showed that women prefer seasonal forecasts to be provided through the extension officer, in a 'teach-in' situation. Results from participatory meetings and household interviews showed that women expressed this preference because they like to ask questions, and also because their time is not flexible enough to be able to sit and listen to a radio programme at a fixed time. Men, in contrast, said that they had no problem scheduling a regular time to listen to a broadcast. This is an important finding, particularly in the light of emphases by practitioners in the forecast community on the development of radio as a means of forecast dissemination. Such an emphasis may exclude a key user group.

There are now a plethora of studies that have looked at the relationship between climate change and women that all reach startlingly similar conclusions:

- Women living in poverty are the most threatened by the dangers that stem from global warming
- Women are largely ignored in climate research, policy and development
- Women are key actors in ensuring their communities' ability to cope with and adapt to climate change

- Women are critical agents of change in communities
- Women's skills and leadership are crucial for people's survival and recovery
- Women's involvement and empowerment are needed to secure sound management of environmental resources
- Women possess initiative, creativity, and capacity to come up with grassroots solutions to adaptation, when they are invested in.

Women's participation in climate change initiatives is often found in NGOs. From Asia, Latin America to Africa, NGOs are supporting women leadership in developing sustainable agriculture, preserving biodiversity, community forestry, securing fresh water supplies, building wind-resistant housing, and more.[33] NGOs have been at the forefront of developing local solutions that embrace women's participation. The answers are not lacking. It is the lack of investment in, and gender blindness to, women's leadership that prevent the scaling-up of gender programmes.

This brief analysis highlights the significance of women's stake in protecting the environment at the local level, in food production, water resource management, and agricultural adaptation. When this stake is ignored projects fail. This suggests that we ignore women's participation in adaptation at our peril.

Current resources are limited, making it even more vital that they are spent effectively. Prioritising the disproportionate burden borne by poor women in the finance of adaptation initiatives will increase the effectiveness and impact of investment. Women's leadership and participation provides a risk management strategy for adaptation investments because of the centrality of their role in household and village life. It ensures that investment reaches those who can have greatest impact on household and village livelihood and therefore reduces the risk of investment failure.

Exploiting opportunities

Adaptation is not just about preparing people to respond to increasing climate hazards; it is also about exploiting opportunities from climate change. One area where exploiting opportunities can be found is in the area of carbon trading. The purpose of carbon trading is to create a market incentive for the world to emit less greenhouse gases than normal. The theory behind carbon trading is based on the need to develop a system that provides the right incentives for greenhouse gas (GHG) reductions and increases the uptake of new emissions-reduction technologies. Enter the global carbon market. The theory suggests that trading in emissions reductions creates a market pull for new clean energy technologies while at the same time putting a price on pollution and thereby providing incentives for people to emit less.[34] The carbon market grew by over 80% in value from US$33 billion in 2006 to $60 billion in 2007.

As carbon markets have grown, so too has criticism of them as a strategy to mitigate climate change. There is now a growing body of evidence to show that carbon markets are inadequate and ineffective in mitigating greenhouse gas emissions.[35] Perhaps the most damning indictment is that whilst the carbon market has doubled year on year since 2005 there has been no equivalent reduction in greenhouse gas emissions. As the carbon market has soared, global greenhouse gas emissions have continued to rise – a stark reminder that a more pragmatic and direct approach to cutting emissions is urgently needed. Relying on international governments to cut greenhouse emissions has to date offered little hope for the peoples of Africa.

In the meantime, Africa needs to get on with adapting. Across the globe entrepreneurial NGOs are beginning to use carbon offsets as a new source of funding for sustainable development in villages. A carbon offset negates or 'neutralises' a ton of CO_2e (carbon dioxide equivalent) emitted in one place by avoiding the release of a ton of CO_2e elsewhere or by sequestering (removing) carbon dioxide from the atmosphere. Carbon offsets are created through various types of projects, such as renewable energy, energy efficiency, destruction of various industrial gases, and carbon sequestration underground or in soils and forests. These carbon projects are meant to benefit global society by avoiding and absorbing excess CO_2 from the atmosphere.

There is now a growing voluntary carbon market where individuals and companies are choosing to offset their emissions by investing in carbon sequestration or emission reduction projects. Carbon markets are enabling additional revenue streams to accrue for project developers who expose and create environmental attributes from the project. Carbon offsets accrue as a result of a project's ability to demonstrate that it lowers greenhouse gas (GHG) emissions. Offsets are traded in carbon credits. One carbon credit demonstrates the reduction of GHGs equal to one metric ton of CO_2e.

The voluntary carbon market is composed of deals that are negotiated on a case-by-case basis. Since the late 1990s, a number of companies (profit and non-profit) have emerged to serve this niche market by funding and managing projects in renewable energy, energy efficiency and forest restoration in developing countries. Voluntary carbon markets have become a fast-growing arena, with some distinct and important advantages for participation of rural communities: [36]

- Products can be highly innovative and flexible
- They can be a source of experimentation and innovation
- They are most likely to reach poorer and smaller communities in developing countries
- They have lower transaction costs
- They can provide up-front finance
- They avoid bureaucratic 'bottlenecks' that plague the CDM
- They can get financing for methodologies not currently approved for sale in the CDM (e.g. avoiding deforestation)
- There is more scope to invest in small-scale projects with high sustainable development
- They open up access to carbon markets for individuals and smaller organisations
- They have potential for development benefits.

A review of 19 carbon sequestration projects in 16 countries in Africa found a range of advantages for the host countries, including increased financial inflows for development. Other benefits included sustainable development, biodiversity conservation, ecological restoration, improved soils and land productivity. Broad estimates from these projects indicate a total potential of approximately 35 million tons of CO_2. Many projects will thus be able to generate carbon credits or offsets. In 2008, the prevailing international prices for carbon credits range from $29.22 a ton at the European Union Trading Scheme to €22.94 for CDM credits. Carbon credits from carbon sequestration projects in Africa are therefore worth potentially millions of dollars.

At the local level carbon trading is also benefiting households. For instance, in the Nhambita Community Carbon Project in Mozambique, each participating household receives a cash payment of $242.60 per hectare over the next seven years (or $34.66 per annum) for carbon sequestered by various land-use activities. This represents a significant increase in most household incomes, and provides access to a regular income source.[37] Similarly, in the International Small Group and Tree Planting Program, Tanzania, local farmers receive regular payments on the basis of the number of trees they can manage on their lands through selling the accrued carbon credits to individuals via e-bay.[38] The Plan Vivo System is another example of carbon trading benefiting rural communities. Plan Vivo works with local NGOs to develop forest management, soil conservation and agricultural improvement. They co-ordinate sales with the offset purchasers and administer payments to local farmers based on the achievement of 'monitoring targets'.[39] In all these examples, NGOs are critical to providing the infrastructure and technological support necessary for village participation.

In terms of developing countries, Africa currently supplies only 3% of the global carbon market. This compares poorly with Asia and Latin America, which contributed 43% and 35%. Although many African carbon sequestration projects are beneficial, expanding them beyond a few pilot schemes needs to address challenges such as tenure insecurity, high transaction costs, political instability and a lack of institutional capacity.[40] Addressing these challenges to scaling up carbon projects is a gap in the market that needs to be filled.

NGOs have a distinct advantage in filling this gap. Companies investing in carbon offsets are driven by profit; NGOs, on the other hand, are driven by development. One of the major criticisms of carbon trading is that it fails to encompass sustainable development. By enabling NGOs to provide the infrastructural support for village participation, it can help to ensure that sustainable development is at the heart of carbon trading, rather than a mere by-product.

The bulk of carbon markets are supplied by credits generated from large-scale national carbon projects in developed countries. However, given the escalation of carbon markets, demand may outstrip supply in the not too distant future. Carbon projects that can provide secure land tenure, transaction costs, technical capacity and institutional infrastructure could go a long way in addressing this potential gap in the market. And again, this is where NGOs come in. They are already stepping up and developing ways to engage communities that enhance rural livelihoods. They are helping to develop the monitoring, administrative, and technical activities that enable small communities to compete with large-scale suppliers of carbon credits. NGOs can provide the structural platform neces-sary to increase village access to carbon trading opportunities, creating an additional income source for local livelihoods. Alternative income sources offer an important adaptation strategy for helping vulnerable communities adapt to climate change. For this reason, in spite of the wealth of criticism relating to carbon trading, it cannot be dismissed as a potential adaptation strategy for NGOs supporting villages in Africa.

Conclusion: the significance of NGOs

This chapter has explored some of the issues that organisations need to consider when addressing climate change in Africa. It identified:

- Climate change scenarios
- Vulnerability
- Adaptation
- Sustainable development
- Gender inequality
- Carbon markets

Future scenarios on the impacts of climate change suggest that in just twelve years' time, millions of people will be affected by the consequences of global warming. Climate exerts significant control over development in Africa. Dependency on rain-fed subsistence agriculture, gender inequality, poverty, and political conflict all undermine developmental resilience in the face of climatic change. Because of its exposure, sensitivity and low adaptive capac-ity, Africa, especially the sub-Saharan region, is especially vulnerable.

Adaptation strategies need to focus on building capacity in villages that address exposure, reduce sensitivity to risk and increase resilience. Reducing vulnerability requires projects that focus on physical impacts as well as the underlying socio-economic, institutional and political factors that determine the capacity of people to respond. Therefore climate change needs to be incorporated into sustainable development initiatives, and sustainable devel-opment initiatives in Africa need to integrate adaptation strategies.

Adaptation happens at the local level, and each area will require its own localised solutions. 70% of Africa's population are in rural areas. Therefore village-level implementation will be critical if adaptation is to reach those most at risk. The proliferation of NGOs at the grassroots level in developing countries highlights an important avenue for providing implementation at the village level. Evidence from the field suggests they have strong networks that can mobilise the infrastructure and technical capacity that is required for village-level adaptation. Their grassroots role provides the community base that is so vital to ensuring adaptation reaches those who are most vulnerable.

Effective adaptation strategies at the village level are built on a foundation of women's leadership and participation. This is because women are responsible for subsistence agriculture and household livelihood in African villages. NGOs that have invested in women's leadership have shown that it can increase impact, scale and intensity of adaptation strategies, helping to save resources and lower the risk of project failure.

Carbon trading is one way in which villages can exploit opportunities from climate change. Although proving to be highly ineffective at reducing greenhouse gas emissions, it is opening up new income flows for sustainable development and adaptation projects. NGOs are playing a leading role in creating the infrastructure and technical support necessary to facilitate access and participation of villages and small communities in carbon trading.

When bringing together this analysis of issues and strategies to respond to them, it highlights the significance of NGOs in delivering adaptation to the most vulnerable populations. NGOs have long been active in capacity building at the grassroots level, and this expertise needs to be integrated into adaptation measures. As this analysis shows, NGOs are already leading the way in supporting communities to adapt to climate change through:

- Women's participation
- Environmental conservation
- Community-based adaptation (CBA)
- Carbon trading

Adaptation requires a community base, localised strategies, women's leadership, self-sufficiency and sustainable development approaches. Therefore, one could argue that the grassroots track record of NGOs makes them the *sine qua non* for adapting to climate change in Africa. If adaptation is to succeed in rural villages across Africa, then NGOs need to be recognised as essential and indispensable actors.

* * *

References

Action Aid (2007) 'Rich governments must pay! Poor people must have a say', Press Release.

W.N. Adger, S. Agrawala, M.M.Q. Mirza, C. Conde, K. O'Brien, J. Pulhin, R. Pulwarty, B. Smit and K. Takahashi (2007) 'Assessment of adaptation practices, options, constraints and capacity' in *Climate Change 2007: Impacts, Adaptation and Vulnerability. Contribution of Working Group II to the Fourth Assessment Report of the Intergovernmental Panel on Climate Change*, M.L. Parry, O.F. Canziani, J.P. Palutikof, P.J. van der Linden and C.E. Hanson, Eds., Cambridge University Press, Cambridge, UK, pp.717-743.

W.N. Adger, N. Brooks, G. Bentham, M. Agnew and S. Eriksen (2004) *New indicators of vulnerability and adaptive capacity*, Tyndall Centre for Climate Change Research, Technical Report 7.

B. Agarwal (2000) 'Conceptualising environmental collective action: Why gender matters' in *Cambridge Journal of Economics*, 24(3), pp.283–310.

L. Aguilar (2007) *Acknowledging the Linkages: Gender and Climate Change*, IUCN-The World Conservation Union.

J. Ayres, M. Grieg-Gran, L. Harris and S. Huq (2006), *Expanding the development benefits from carbon offsets*, International Institute for Environment and Development, London.

S. Baden (1999) 'Practical strategies for involving women as well as men in water and sanitation activities', Bridge Development-Gender, Institute of Development Studies, UK.

R. Bayon, A. Hawn and K. Hamilton (2007) *Voluntary Carbon Markets*, Earthscan, UK.

M. Boko, I. Niang, A. Nyong, C. Vogel, A. Githeko, M. Medany, B. Osman-Elasha, R. Tabo and P. Yanda (2007) 'Africa' in *Climate Change 2007: Impacts, Adaptation and Vulnerability. Contribution of Working Group II to the Fourth Assessment Report of the Intergovernmental Panel on Climate Change*, M.L. Parry, O.F. Canziani, J.P. Palutikof, P.J. van der Linden and C.E. Hanson, Eds., Cambridge University Press, Cambridge UK, pp.433-467.

I. Burton, S. Huq, B. Lim, O. Pilifosova and E.L. Schipper (2002) 'From Impacts Assessment to Adaptation Priorities: the Shaping of Adaptation Policy' in *Climate Policy* 2(2002), pp.145-159.

Carbon Trade Watch (2007) *The Carbon Neutral Myth: Offset Indulgences for your Climate Sins*, The Transnational Institute, Amsterdam.

CBA-X (2006) Community-Based Adaptation Exchange, www.cba-exchange.org/

FAO (2004) *Gender and Food Security*, UN Food and Agriculture Organisation, www.fao.org/Gender/en/agri-e.htm (accessed 10/05/08).

J. Fisher (1998) *Nongovernments: NGOs and Political Development of the Third World*, Kumarian Press, Connecticut, USA.

J. Ford (2008) 'Emerging Trends in Climate Change Policy: The Role of Adaptation' in *International Public Policy Review* Volume 3, Number 2.

K. Hamilton, R. Bayon, G. Turner, D. Higgins (2007) *State of the Voluntary Carbon Markets 2007: Picking Up Steam*, New Carbon Finance and Ecosystems Marketplace, UK and USA.

E. Harris (2006) *The Voluntary Carbon Market: Current and Future Market Status and Implications for Development Benefits*, IIED and New Economics Foundation, London.

A. Hawn (2005) 'eBay Shoppers and Subsistence Farmers Meet on Virtual Ground' in Ecosystem Market Place, October 5, 2005.

M. Holman (2007) 'Are There Any Benefits of Non-Governmental Organisations (NGOs) in Kenya?' Kenya Environmental and Political News Weblog http://kenvironews.wordpress.com.

S. Huq and H. Reid (2007) Community-Based Adaptation: an IIED Briefing, International Institute for Environment and Development, London, UK.

IRC (1999) Vulnerability and capacity assessment – An International Federation Guide, International Federation of Red Cross and Red Crescent Societies, Switzerland.

R. Jindal (2006) Carbon Sequestration Projects in Africa: Potential Benefits and Challenges to Scaling Up, EarthTrends 2006, World Resources Institute.

S.J. Klees (2008) 'NGOs, Civil Society, and Development: Is There a Third Way' in Current Issues in Comparative Education, Vol 10(1/2), pp.22-25.

L. Lohmann (2006) 'Carbon Trading: a critical conversation on climate change, privatisation and power', in Development Dialogue no.48, September 2006, The Dag Hammarskjöld Centre, Sweden.

Madre (2008) A Women's Rights-based Approach to Climate Change, Madre, New York, USA. www.madre.org/articles/int/climatechange.html (accessed 8/05/08).

T. Mitchell, T. Tanner and K. Lussier (2007) We know what we need – South Asian women speak out on climate change adaptation, Action Aid and The Institute of Development Studies (IDS), UK.

R. Nampinga (2008) Gender Perspectives on Climate Change, Commission on the Status of Women, Fifty-second session New York, 25 February-7 March 2008, United Nations.

C. Nhemachena and R. Hassan (2007) 'Micro-Level Analysis of Farmers' Adaptation to Climate Change in Southern Africa', FPRI Discussion Paper 00714 August 2007, Food Policy Research Institute, Washington, USA.

C. Nhemachena, R. Hassan and J. Benhin (2006) Assessment of farmers' adaptation strategies to climate change in Southern Africa, UN Framework on Climate Change COP-12, Adaptation and Development Days, Nairobi, Kenya, 11-12 November 2006.

Oxfam (2007) 'Financing adaptation: why the UN's Bali Climate Conference must mandate the search for new funds', Oxfam Briefing Note 2007.

S. Pagiola, J. Bishop and N. Landell-Mills (eds.) (2002) Selling Forest Environmental Services, Earthscan Publications, London, UK.

T. Prato (2008) 'Accounting for risk and uncertainty in determining preferred strategies for adapting to future climate change' in Mitigation and Adaptation Strategies for Global Change, Volume 13, Number 1, January 2008.

K.D. Reimann (2006) 'A View from the Top: International Politics, Norms and the Worldwide Growth of NGOs', International Studies Quarterly (2006) 50, pp.45–67.

S. Riordan (2000) 'Put Your Money Where Your Mouth Is: Public Funding of Women's Organisations', in Gender and Development, Volume 8 Number 1, March 2000, pp.63-70.

S.H. Schneider, S. Semenov, A. Patwardhan, I. Burton, C.H.D. Magadza, M. Oppenheimer, A.B. Pittock, A. Rahman, J.B. Smith, A. Suarez and F. Yamin (2007) 'Assessing key vulnerabilities and the risk from climate change' in Climate Change 2007: Impacts, Adaptation and Vulnerability. Contribution of Working Group II to the

Fourth Assessment Report of the Intergovernmental Panel on Climate Change, M.L. Parry, O.F. Canziani, J.P. Palutikof, P.J. van der Linden and C.E. Hanson, Eds., Cambridge University Press, Cambridge, UK, pp.779-810.

N. Stern (2007) *The Economics of Climate Change: The Stern Review*, Cambridge University Press, UK.

N. Taiyab (2006) *Exploring the market for voluntary carbon offsets*, International Institute for Environment and Development, London.

UNEP/GRID (2006) 'Emissions of carbon dioxide, in Africa and selected OECD countries', United Nations Environment Programme/GRID-Arendal, http://maps.grida.no.

WWF-UK (2007) *Emission Impossible: access to JI/CDM credits in phase II of the EU Emissions Trading Scheme*, World Wildlife Fund, UK.

Notes

1. The research was completed as part of the Msc in Sustainable Development and Environmental Change at the University of Exeter. An extensive bibliography from the research is available direct from the author.

2. Reimann 2006, p.45.

3. Fisher 1998, p.6.

4. Schneider et al 2007, p.791.

5. Burton et al 2002, p.155.

6. See especially Stern Review 2007, pp.104-137.

7. Adger et al 2007, p.719.

8. Action Aid 2007.

9. Aguilar, 2007, p.3.

10. FAO 2004.

11. Mehretu and Mutambira (1992), cited in Nampinga 2008.

12. Action Aid 2007, p.2.

13. Boko et al 2007, p.452.

14. Nhemachena and Hassan 2007, p.8.

15. Adger et al 2004, p.6.

16. Ford 2008, p.11.

17. UNEP/GRID 2006.

18. Oxfam 2007, p.1.

19. Huq and Reid 2007, p.1.

20. IRC 1999, p.12.

21. Fisher 1998, p.5.

22. Union of International Associations' Yearbook of International Organisations.

23. Neoliberalism is a theory of political economic practice that proposes that human well-being can best be advanced by liberating individual entrepreneurial freedoms and skills within an institutional framework characterised by strong private property rights, free markets and free trade.

24. See especially Klees 2008 for analysis of this argument.

25. Holman 2007.
26. Reimann 2006, p.64.
27. Fisher 1998, p.6.
28. See especially CBA-X 2008 and also The 2nd International Workshop on Community-Based Adaptation (CBA) to Climate Change www.iisd.ca/ymb/sdban.
29. Huq and Reid 2007, p.1.
30. Nhemachena and Hassan 2007, p.vi.
31. Agarwal 2000, p.305.
32. See for example, Riordan 2000.
33. See for example, Baden 1999, Madre 2008, Mitchell et al 2008.
34. Bayon et al, 2007, p.3.
35. See especially Carbon Trade Watch 2007, Lohmann 2006, WWF-UK 2007.
36. See especially, Ayres et al 2006, Harris 2006, Taiyab 2006.
37. Jindal 2006, p.2.
38. Hawn 2005.
39. See Pagiola et al 2002.
40. See Jindal 2006.

Chapter Three

Global education as sustainable community education: stories from Brazil, the Middle East and Albania

by David Selby

Varieties of global education

Towards the close of a Regional Conference on Global Education organised by UNICEF MENA (Middle East and North Africa) and held at Broumana in Lebanon in July 1995, I was asked, as conference consultant, to prepare at short notice a transparency conveying the essence of global education. For better or worse, I presented delegates with the following:

> Global Education is a holistic paradigm of education predicated upon the interconnectedness of communities, lands and peoples, the interrelatedness of all social, cultural and natural phenomena, the interpenetrative nature of past, present and future, and the complementary nature of the cognitive, affective, physical and spiritual dimensions of the human being, It addresses issues of development, equity, peace, social and environmental justice, and environmental sustainability. Its scope encompasses the personal, the local, the national and the planetary. Congruent with its precepts and principles, its pedagogy is experiential, interactive, learner-centred, democratic, convivial, participatory and change-oriented.

> It needs to be said that there are multiple interpretations and varieties of global education, and that the term continues to be subject to the same kind of 'semantic inflation' that Lucie Sauvé identifies in the discourses of sustainable development and its educational manifestations.[1]

There are those who conceive global education as an educational expression of what they see – and applaud – as the globalisation imperative. This rendition of global education, sometimes referred to as 'global competitiveness education',[2] is about equipping the learner with the skills and competencies for proactive engagement in global society and for achieving competitive advantage in the global marketplace. It embraces globalisation as a given; emphasises education for purposes of economic development and social cohesion, conceiving of the latter as a *sine qua non* of robust economic performance. It has a strong knowledge and skills emphasis, but de-emphasises exploration of values and assumptions. Offering a by and large 'business as usual' pro-consumerist view of the world, it tends to offer a 'band aid' critique of the global condition.[3]

Global education that falls within what Toh Swee Hin calls the 'liberal-technocratic paradigm of global literacy' offers a somewhat sturdier reformist agenda.[4] It is characterised by a liberal idealist appreciation of other cultures and cultural diversity, while often treating 'culture' superficially and leaving the voice of the 'other' and the authenticity of learner feelings towards the 'other', largely unexplored and unexpressed. It emphasises the interdependent nature of the world, the world as 'system' rather than 'collection' of lands and peoples, but falls short of rigorously addressing the exploitative and, hence, asymmetrical, nature of global interdependencies. It brings a management and technocratic lens to addressing the imbalances in the global system and the deleterious environmental and social impacts of globalisation, favouring what Toh Swee Hin calls 'technocratic social engineering upon planet Earth', an approach commensurate with the interests of the powerful. "When deconstructed," Toh writes, "this technocratic notion of interdependence is essentially self-centred. Selfish-interest is the bottom line and those already well-off in the planetary hierarchy require understanding of world affairs to cope with the problems of system disequilibria."[5] Failing to comprehensively embrace 'global literacy for emancipation and justice', it is marked by uncritical assumptions concerning the inexorability of human progress (with progress implicitly or explicitly understood as powered by unbridled economic growth and continuing high levels of mass consumption). In short, it embraces a paradigm and associated values set that are directed at tinkering with, rather than turning around, the global condition. As such, liberal reformist expressions of global education more or less align with mainstream renditions of education for sustainable development where economic growth and globalisation are tacitly, if not explicitly, embraced and an internationalist management and technocratic view of what to do with the world predominates.[6]

Transformative global education, the essence of which my Broumana definition, cited earlier, grasped at capturing, seeks to adopt an explicitly and rigorously ethical position, making the values and dispositions of holism, emancipation, liberation and empowerment central to the learning experience, applying them to what are seen as mutually-embedded personal, social and political realms. Its proponents call for a conscious attempt to link the deepening of an individual's interior life to solidarity with, as well as participation in, crucial struggles for justice, dignity and freedom. *Inter alia* they advocate: a confronting of structural violence and of structural hypocrisy and denial as vital for planetary survival; addressing processes of marginalisation and exclusion through giving prominence to the voice of the marginalised and excluded; making ecological security and the intrinsic valuing of the other-than-human integral to both liberation and well-being; a conscientising and empowering pedagogy involving the progressive spreading of leadership across any learning community.[7]

A four-dimensional model of global education

A holistic, transformative disposition helped inspire the model of global education informing the initiatives storied in the coming pages.

The four-dimensional model (see Fig.1 on next page) was developed in the late 1980s at the Centre for Global Education, University of York, but was put to concrete effect through the developing world partnerships of the International Institute for Global Education, University of Toronto, between 1992 and 2003. It comprises three outer dimensions and an inner dimension, reflecting what are seen as the complementary goals of enabling the learner to engage with the world while exploring their inner, personal world or 'inscape'. All four dimensions are seen as profoundly interrelated.

The *spatial dimension* addresses the concepts of interdependence and interconnectedness at multiple levels including the intrapersonal, interpersonal, local, bioregional, national, international and global. The levels are not conceived mechanistically as concentric circles with world furthest from self but as mutually enfolded and in dynamic relationship. An event at any level can reverberate through, and significantly affect, all other levels, feeding back through the whole so as to further transform the level and point of origin. In this way, it is both unhelpful and misguided to dichotomise local and global, just as other dichotomies spawned by the prevailing mechanistic worldview need to be revisited through a holistic

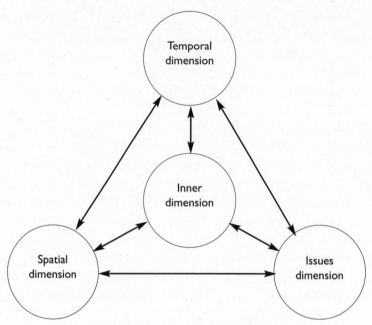

Figure 3.1: The four dimensions of global education

lens to transformative effect: for instance, nature/culture; human/animal; mind/body; ordinary/extraordinary; sacred/profane; reason/emotion; content/process.

The *issues dimension* calls for learners to explore key global themes and issues, each of which will be manifest at all levels, including the personal and local, the intention being to bring community into classroom and take learning out into the community. Umbrella themes include: culture, economy, environment, equity, health, needs/rights, peace, social justice and sustainability. In engaging with a theme or issue, the learner is challenged to consider diverse perspectives through a variety of cultural, disciplinary, social, ideological and paradigmatic lenses. S/he is also encouraged to view themes and issues holistically. Hence, a major 'environmental problem' needs to be viewed as inevitably folded into a panoply of other issues, for instance, raw materials shortages and price rises, rising unemployment, widening disparities between rich and poor, rising levels of psychiatric illness, and regional conflict. 'Problems' are thus conceived as arising from multi-layered webs of relations between themes, while 'solutions' come to be viewed as provisional adjustments within an ongoing, dynamic process, having in turn their own problem-fomenting effect.

The *temporal dimension* concerns raising awareness of the co-creating and co-evolving nature of past, present and future, with consequent illuminations for understandings and actions. It is also about bringing a futures dimension to learning, a dimension paradoxically missing from schools, universities and informal learning contexts tasked with educating for the future. Futures-oriented learning concerns *probable, possible* and *preferred* futures (respectively, futures that are *likely to come about,* that *might conceivably come about* and that *we would like to have realised*). In galvanizing institutions and communities for change, the future is depicted as a *zone of potential,* in which futures that we prefer but that presently stand at the margins of the zone can be pushed, through our own actions, to the centre of the zone. To do this, we need to facilitate futures-oriented learning contexts that produce 'practical visionaries', that is learners with renewed vision possessing the capacities and disposition to help realise and actualise that vision.

The *inner dimension* recognises the dynamic and complementary relationship, the relational holism,[8] between an individual's inner and outer worlds. Drawing upon insights from the quantum world, the model sees a 'dance' between 'inner' and 'outer' world in which our self-awareness, self-perception and sense of identity are profoundly influenced by our understanding of events in the world while a centred sense of self heightens our proactivity in seeking to affect the world for the better.[9]

The inner dimension, in particular, but also the four dimensions taken together, point to a pedagogy that:

- Facilitates interaction, participation and experiential, including action-oriented, learning
- Enables learners to explore values, assumptions, perspectives, hopes and fears in a challenging but affirming context
- Fosters co-operative and collaborative attitudes and skills
- Builds individual and group self-confidence and self-esteem, both cornerstones of personal and community empowerment
- Nurtures intuition, emotion, imagination, sensory awareness and embodied learning as vital complements to the epistemologically under-dimensioned menu of much school-age and adult learning, straitjacketed as they are by rational, analytical and knowledge-grounded means of knowing.[10]

It has been a significant feature of the transformative global education approach that it has sought to concretise its curricular and pedagogical proposals by providing a wide range of activities that teachers in the formal sector as well as those facilitating community learning can readily employ. Their use is equally important for facilitator development, in that those animating such processes need themselves to have experienced and become sensitised to their learning potential.[11]

Narratives of engagement in developing-world formal and non-formal community-transformation initiatives informed by the four-dimensional model, and employing its associated pedagogies, follow.

A Canadian/Brazilian convergence for community transformation

Núcleo Internacional de Educação e Gestão Ambiental (NIEGA) is a not-for-profit non-governmental organisation established in São Paulo, Brazil, in 1993 with the goal of promoting 'an environmental ethic comprising socially and environmentally responsible action by means of transformative global learning oriented towards active and transformative participation in every sphere of social life'.[12] Between 1993 and 2003 it was in active partnership with the International Institute for Global Education of the University of Toronto in taking forward an International Training for Environmental Leadership (ITEL) initiative as well as linked global education capacity building programmes for Brazilian municipalities and communities, businesses and non-governmental organisations.

ITEL involved giving Brazilian environmental leaders, often economically disadvantaged and normally unable to afford travel, access to an international experience hosted on a free-of-charge basis by Canadian public bodies, non-governmental organisations and higher education institutions in Toronto and Montreal (subsidies for travel were oftentimes wrestled out of airlines and corporations; costs were kept to a minimum, with participants paying what they could). Ten visits to Canada took place between 1993 and 2002, each visit sandwiched between self-organised preparatory and follow-up sessions in Brazil. 127 participants went through the ITEL programme, 90% being women.[13] The Brazil-based sessions and Canadian programme attempted "what could be called a radical form of inclusion and collaboration" by employing a global education philosophy and methodology aimed at enabling "Brazilian participants to value their own experiences in the field of education for the environment, for citizenship and for social change".[14] The objectives of ITEL, writes Marli Santos, the initiative co-ordinator, were to:

> collaborate with participants in their non-formal, continuing education, and to promote awareness of environmental issues in a global perspective, that is to develop world-mindedness. The programme also aims to empower participants to comprehend, realise and utilise their full potential, and to develop confidence and self-esteem in order to promote positive actions for social and environmental change.[15]

Santos perceives a 'spiritual dimension' guiding the programme:

> What is meant by spirituality . . . is awareness and exercise of the values of compassion, love, justice, co-operation, generosity and solidarity. It is also a process of expanding the small sense of self towards the large Self, of seeing the essential connections between others, humans as well as other-than-human, and us.[16]

Linked to the ITEL programme was a series of one-week 'international' global education workshops in São Paulo (September 1995, April 1997 and March 2001) co-facilitated by the academics from the International Institute for Global Education (IIGE). The workshops were framed according to the four-dimensional model and were designed to give participants, primarily drawn from Brazilian non-governmental organisations, an intense experience of global education learning processes combined with reflection on using the processes in their social-change initiatives.

The strong support network developed amongst participants in the ITEL experience and the IIGE/NIEGA São Paulo workshops, as well as the continuous and consistent advocacy and activism of NIEGA personnel, prompted a plethora of community transformation initiatives. Brief stories of three such initiatives are told below.

Story One: Bringing environmental concern to a social housing agency through grassroots action

The governmental social housing agency in question is in charge of providing low-income housing within the State of São Paulo and is considered one of the largest public housing agencies in the world. The employee originator of (hitherto unsuccessful) attempts to infuse environmentalism into agency strategy came into contact with NIEGA and its global education programme in 1997. An emerging understanding of the holistic and systemic underpinnings of global education, as well as growing familiarity with its learning approaches, enabled her, from small beginnings, to build a cumulatively influential series of seminars and workshops for professionals and support staff from various sectors of the agency. Altogether, some seventy educational events, informed by the four-dimensional model, and including specific global education workshops, were held between 1997 and 2000, aimed at promoting discussion and action around applying sustainability and 'clean production' principles to popular housing. There were altogether 2,809 participants, their experience of a 'participatory, interactive and inclusive process of teaching and learning' being crucial in provoking 'changes at personal, interpersonal and structural levels within the organisation'. The swell of sustainability consciousness within the agency, catalyzed in part by 22 agency workers who had participated in ITEL, led to the establishment of an Environmental Management Department in October 1999 tasked with the mission of continuing the environmental sensitisation programme, incorporating environmental variables into decision-making, applying Agenda 21 to the agency's sphere of activity, and "promoting the principles of sustainability and clean production for renewing public housing policy of the state of São Paulo". A specific goal of the Department is concerned with "consolidating the methodology and principles of global education, as basic instruments to promote changes in social values, attitudes and behaviours". Another concrete outcome of the educational programme, starting in the year 2000, was the development by a team of some 80 agency professionals of a pilot project in eco-design for popular housing, seeking to "simultaneously incorporate principles of global education, healthy communities, clean production and socio-environmental responsibility".[17]

Story Two: Saving the mangrove with global education

This story concerns a large, environmentally responsible mining company based in the State of Espírito Santo that lies along the Atlantic south-east coast of Brazil. With a track record of supporting environmental education programmes for employees and local communities, the company took up in 2003 a 'Save the Sea' initiative proposed by a fisherman concerned about the impact of oil spills on the integrity and fecundity of the local mangrove. The practice by local fishermen and owners of tourist boats of releasing used oil in small but constant amounts on return to port was proving not only ecologically damaging but also prejudicial to the economic activities of fishing (the mangroves being the fish breeding grounds) and tourism itself.

The mechanism for changing the habit was simple enough to determine, and cheap enough to implement, the company readily agreeing to recover the oil and sell the recycled oil to the boatmen at a token price.

The contribution of global education was significant in helping further embed a pro-social, pro-environmental ethos in the thinking and behaviours of the mining company executive and its staff, and subsequently in informing the content and process of an environmental education course for fishermen.

At the company's 2002 Environmental Week, the (male) miners and mining managers attended a workshop on global education, in which interactive learning was employed to elicit participants' needs in terms of hard information on environmental issues having a direct bearing on local community quality of life, as well as their ideas for environmental campaigns around which they could mobilise. As the co-ordinator of the company's environmental education programme, a participant in the 2001 ITEL programme in Canada, stated:

> One example of the importance of global education methodology, which is interactive and change-oriented, was the high level of involvement of our staff during this workshop in June 2002. It was interesting to see the motivation and participation of the entire group during this workshop. People that almost never speak before the boss were very comfortable in reflecting upon their activities and making suggestions for future improvements.[18]

The subsequent responsiveness to the lone fisherman, facilitators felt, was informed by the workshop experience and the pooling and discussion of environmental campaign ideas that took place. According to the co-ordinator:

> One thousand fishermen have registered for the project and about 100 have participated in an environmental education course organised by the mining company on the repercussions of oil spills on coastal environments. In this community, 263 boats operated by 400 fishermen stopped discarding oil at sea, in the mangroves and on the beach.[19]

"Global education's contribution to this project," Santos concludes, "has been to provide its originator (the environmental education co-ordinator) with a methodology and theoretical framework for implementing the idea of educating the whole person, by addressing the intellectual, emotional, physical, moral and spiritual dimensions of the learner in a holistic way. Interactive learning methods that encourage co-operation, solidarity, dialogue and active participation are strong components in the pedagogy applied in the 'Save our Sea' project."[20]

Story Three: A municipal global education initiative for 'at risk' youth

Project Polis was taken up by a São Paulo municipality in 2000 as its contribution to a 'regional social commitment network', a term underscoring the importance of all social actors working together for the well-being of youth. It is a 'complementary education' programme for youth aged 12-19 years, aimed at developing basic citizenship skills, improving employability, developing interpersonal skills and enhancing leisure skills. It was distinctive in that its programme brought together delinquent youth attached to state institutions, 'at risk' street youth from the city and other young people, an approach that initially elicited strong public opposition that had to be weathered by the municipal authority.

Encountering global education in late 2000, the Project Polis co-ordinator arranged for its community leaders and some adolescents to participate in a range of ITEL and NIEGA global education workshops over the next several months, including the International Institute for Global Education 'international' workshop in São Paulo in March 2001 focusing on citizenship issues, social action, and social and environmental justice issues.

In July 2001 the municipality entered an official partnership with NIEGA and early in 2002 a rolling programme of monthly six-hour Project Polis global education workshops for community leaders, facilitated by NIEGA staff, plus weekly two-hour discussion group sessions, was initiated.

The impact of a cumulative programme of global education learning experiences was powerful. For the Project Polis co-ordinator, global education immersion opened up the connection between social and environmental issues: "We felt that the connections between these two areas could open up new perspectives on our work in the social area, especially in relation to our work with adolescents." [21] A colleague concurred:

> When I first heard about global education, I saw that we had here an approach to deal with the exclusion of the poorest population from the market. We had the idea to work with recycling, not only because it creates jobs, but also because this work touches upon many concepts and will have a significant impact in the social, environmental and economic areas. Questions such as: What to do? How will the impacts multiply? What are the interconnections with issues such as water resources, health, poverty, inequality, citizenship? All this had a significant impact on my work in the social area of municipal government and personal development. [22]

Community leaders thus realised that the primary challenge of global education concerned how to animate the development of a broad and connected awareness amongst the youth with whom they worked. One global education activity reported as of significance in this regard was 'Woolly Thinking', an activity involving teams in negotiating connections between different global and social issues, a circle of 'static negotiators', one per team, being connected by yarn following each successful negotiation. [23] This highly tactile and kinesthetic learning device, heavily overlaid with symbolic learning potential as the web of connection emerges, proved to be resonant with meaning for disadvantaged groups of youths as they tackled and connected issues such as drugs, ill-health, violence, gender inequality, poverty, pollution and social exclusion as present in their lives. The connecting of issues through this and other activities, together with processes of exploring the personal or 'inner' dimension with a view to developing adolescent's potential for creativity and pro-social risk-taking, led to a range of concrete initiatives that engaged youth by directly addressing their real issues.

Santos reports concrete outcomes of the Project Polis global education partnership as including:

- A flourishing Project Polis youth choir with a repertoire devoted to building a culture of peace

- The opening of a volunteer-run language centre to develop the communication skills of youths, allied to which is an environmental arts-based programme of drama, mask and language workshops designed to give voice to participants and develop their proactive citizenship skills

- A post 9/11 municipal peace education initiative for youth designed to build a critical perspective on the present and future state of the planet and addressing social and environmental degradation, intolerance and under-privilege

- A focus through the above-outlined initiatives on cultivating the creativity, self-esteem, confidence, and pro-social risk-taking dispositions of participants.[24]

For one community leader, a signal success of the initiatives was the successful bringing together and co-involvement on an equal footing of youth 'who are needy, those who are at-risk' and institutionally attached, 'at risk' street youth having no attachment to a state institution, and visiting youth not 'at risk', resulting in a turnaround in initially hostile media and public perceptions of the Polis scheme.[25]

Global education, school and community in the Middle East and Albania

From 1993-8 the International Institute for Global Education (IIGE) was engaged on a consultancy and facilitation basis by UNICEF MENA in a Global Education Initiative in Jordan and Lebanon in conjunction with the Ministries of Education of the two countries. The aim of the Initiative was to advance national curriculum and pedagogical renewal of basic education for grades 5 to 10 framed within the global education four-dimensional model, and to develop linked pre-service and in-service teacher education programmes. In Jordan, the Initiative was set within the national Educational Reform Plan that formed part of the process of democratisation inspired by the late King Hussein. In Lebanon, the Initiative took place against the backcloth of the civil war of 1975-89, a period during which curriculum and school development were frozen. In both countries the Initiative involved identifying windows of opportunity for the infusion of global education themes (such as environment, futures, human rights and peace) into the national curriculum; a move away from predominantly transmissive teaching (and passive learning) through the implementation of interactive learning; the production of student and teacher support materials; and the training of teacher educators and teachers of the pilot schools in the facilitation of interactive and participatory learning approaches as well as change agency and change advocacy skills.[26]

The dissemination of the Initiative within the region, not least through regional gatherings such as the Broumana conference referred to earlier, led to collaboration in similar schemes by UNICEF, IIGE and the respective Ministry of Education in Syria (1995-2004) and Iran (2000-4). Outside the region the approach was picked up in the UNICEF-funded 1998-2001 Albanian Global Education Project for grades 5, 6 and 7, involving the Albanian Institute of Pedagogical Studies (the curriculum, teaching and learning arm of the Ministry of Education) and IIGE, and the UNICEF 1998-2001 grade 1-10 Life Skills Curriculum Development Project in Armenia. These initiatives were followed by the 2001-4 UNICEF CARK (Central Asian Republics and Kazakhstan) Global Education Project aimed at developing new curricula and interactive pedagogies for grade 1-10 students in the five republics of Central Asia.

In each Initiative a national core team was formed, a group of experienced country-based curriculum developers, classroom practitioners and representatives of human rights, anti-poverty and environmental not-for-profit organisations working in conjunction with the IIGE team. Their role was to advise on national and school culture, ensure the cultural appropriateness of the curriculum, learning activities and learning materials developed, and to play a progressively more prominent role in curriculum and pedagogical development, teacher training and evaluation (with commensurate phased reduction of IIGE involvement and profile). The IIGE team, for its part, had the role of training the core team in curriculum development (including subject integration), the facilitation of interactive learning, and framing and instigating the project evaluation; also, as the core team acquired capacity and assumed a greater leadership role, returning occasionally to undertake a periodic assessment with the eye of a 'critical friend'.[27]

Other than meeting together during the visits of IIGE staff, the core team and Institute members communicated through long-distance exchange and dialogue around new sets of activities drawing upon and conflating the four dimensions of the global education model. At the outset IIGE would forward sets of proposed grade-specific activities, on which the core team would give feedback according to learner, school culture and wider cultural appropriateness. As the capacity and confidence of the core team grew, they would devise and forward their activity sets, in response to which IIGE team members would offer thematic and pedagogical suggestions. This proved a worthwhile, if burdensome, process.

What follows are stories from two of the UNICEF projects of school and community change and engagement arising from school-based curriculum development.

Story Four: Dislodging perceptual barriers in Lebanese schools and communities

Successive evaluations of the Global Education Initiative in Lebanon suggest a significant disruption of the perceptions of teachers, students and community members attached to the pilot schools (17 originally, rising to 72 and spread across the country).

Experiencing the new facilitative-style learning, the vast majority of students expressed enjoyment about an approach that gave them opportunities to work collaboratively, express opinions freely and contribute actively. While some encountered 'pedagogical culture shock'[28] at what they saw as the disorder and chaos of the active lessons, a more common sentiment was that the new learning facilitated the assimilation of information and helped deepen understandings. Some students expressed surprise about the galvanizing impact of the activities on peers previously regarded as shy, work-disinclined or under-achieving. They also expressed fascination that it was possible to learn through linking subjects together. The sharing and greater openness inherent in active learning seems to have enabled teachers to come across as real people more effectively than they had before and to establish close bonds with their students. "Activity learning strengthens affectionate ties between me and my teacher," wrote one student from the Mount Lebanon area.[29]

In terms of learning achievement, the primary gains were in terms of life skills and attitudinal development. Across the lifetime of the Initiative, teachers and evaluators in Lebanon (and Jordan) attested to student accomplishments in expressing opinions, active listening, discussion and argument, consensus building, creative thinking and accommodating to alternative perspectives.[30] While the experiential nature of the learning helped students internalise concepts, the approach was less effective in terms of learning definitions and scientific and technical terminology so that achievement in traditional assessment (primarily factual recall) terms did not significantly increase.[31]

A major outcome of teacher involvement in the Global Education Initiative was a shift, often quite radical, in their perception of their role. As the Lebanese core team reported: "The long years of the civil war had deprived them of any personal or professional development. The methodology allowed them to think positively of themselves and their work."[32] While many found it hard to avoid old habits of over-directing students, and their debriefing of learning experiences tended to be on the rushed side, remaining oftentimes insufficiently responsive to student input, teachers did succeed in adopting a more facilitative, humane and democratic role and persona, to the obvious appreciation and delight of students, and bringing about a sea-change in the climate of both classroom and school.

Teachers also proved highly adaptable. Most teachers had anticipated problems in implementing activities because of conditions existing in their schools such as inadequate classroom space, large class size, and heavy and hard-to-move furniture. As things turned out, teachers proved remarkably inventive in finding alternative spaces and in accommodating to the space available so that interactive learning could happen. As consultant, I watched one Lebanese grade five teacher use the playground for a silent, co-operative 'map of Lebanon' learning drama. A huge map of Lebanon, with north, south, east and west indicated, had been drawn on the tarmac. Students closed their eyes and had a paper with the name of a city, town, mountain range, valley or river name pinned to their back. Opening their eyes and without speaking, they each had to place and juxtapose themselves within the chalk map, 'river' students forming meandering shapes on the tarmac and 'mountain' students raising arms in body sculptures. I watched another grade five teacher use the same technique in another school playground using a large outline of a human body in which students had to help each other locate the body part they represented.

Gender conventions and perceptions were also somewhat eroded by the Initiative. While the tradition of boys and girls sitting in separate rows or blocks in class tended to continue, sexes mixed for interactive and experiential activities with increasing comfort levels. The lessons, reported teachers in West Beirut, had "helped in breaking the gender barrier as students showed more willingness to mingle", a sentiment echoed by teachers in most pilot schools.[33]

As the project unfolded, there were increasing calls for involving parents and other members of the adult community as full partners in the Initiative. This did not happen in any systematic way, probably because the logistics seemed too steep a mountain to climb. It was left to other country projects, such as in Albania, to exploit the community potential more fully. Parents did express pride that their school was a pilot school for such an innovative project, and there is ample evidence of frequent 'round the table' evening conversations arising from children raising issues discussed in class and relating their experiences of the new learning. They, and fellow community members, were drawn in as learning periodically spilled out of the pilot school classrooms in pursuance of environmental projects such as stream and beach clearing, community questionnaire surveys, and the eliciting of adult views on possible, probable and preferred futures.[34]

Story Five: Global education, Roma, refugees and blood feuds in Albania

In the Albanian Global Education Project, the new grade five to seven classroom learning spilled out into the 26 participating schools and their communities.

The principal and teachers at Ramazan Jarani School, set in an economically impoverished and multi-ethnic district of the Albanian capital, Tirana, saw early on the opportunities offered by the curriculum and pedagogical aspects of the Project for effecting whole-school change through building school/community links. Murals on the rights of the child on the inner walls of the school were the outcome of one school project that brought teachers, students, parents and other community members together. Parents and other adults cleaned up and took care of the walls outside the school, and repaired and refurbished the fountain at the entrance to the school, the principal reporting that vandalism had ceased. Through their labours, the community supported the building of a greenhouse as part of a 'green school' project, and furnished the school with plants. Students started a school/community newsletter for young people and then supported the community in starting and distributing its own newsletter. Newsletter proceeds were used to buy and install water pipes for the greenhouse. Community and parent representatives became involved in democratised school decision-making processes. A community centre was established within the school, and community exhibitions periodically held.[35] Another significant element of what was a transformational process was the attention paid using global education anti-discriminatory and conflict-resolution processes to dismantling negative images of the indigenous Roma community whose children formed some 80% of the school population. Roma girls in the community were frequently the victims of sex trafficking, so as an extension of the global education approach, trafficking-protection life-skills lessons were given in co-operation with the Albanian YMCA. "The global education dimensions," the principal asserted, "are not an 'extra' separate subject in the national curriculum but they are concepts that are integrated inside current curricula and outside school walls." [36]

I will recount my own visit to the school in September 2000. I received a conducted tour of the school and grounds by a very proud community leader who waxed enthusiastically about the school's greening, child rights, school democracy and anti-discriminatory initiatives. Duly inspired and impressed, in thanking him I asked him what his occupation was. "Oh, a member of secret police," he replied!

During the Kosovo refugee crisis of 1999, the Albanian global education pilot schools became collection centres offering refugee children assistance and protection. Albanian teachers from the schools trained Kosovar teachers on using global education activities to help heal traumatised children and adults in refugee camps, themselves helping out with (and role modelling) the learning. As Lidra Remacka, one of the Albanian core team members recalls with some emotion:

> One of my unforgettable stories comes from the refugee camp of summer 1999. Albanian teachers were unprepared to explain the meaning of the word 'enemy'. For Kosovar children enemy means 'Serbs' because they saw their houses burned,

their grandparents killed, but it's not the same meaning for Albanian children who have only heard about Serbs. Using global education philosophy, especially the temporal and inner dimensions, through art therapy, global education teachers tried to touch children's feelings and parents' emotions in the camp.[37]

Another important community issue in remote areas, steeped in Albania's past, is that of inter-familial blood feuds and vendettas, especially in the north of the country, where family 'honour' is held to have been tarnished. The issue came to the fore within the Global Education Project when an anonymous letter was received by the principal of the high school in Lezha, a northern city with a hard core blood feud tradition, requesting that teachers of the school use global education conflict resolution approaches as a way of stopping blood feuds in the community.[38] Global education workshops were held for both male parents and children on the blood feud issue. For the former, guided visualisation techniques based on Albanian writings on blood feuds, were employed to provoke discussion among some fifty men involved in or affected by vendettas. For the latter, children of victim and perpetrator families undertook art therapy and trust activities as a means of bringing concerns, fears, resentments and guilt feelings into the open and identifying positive ways forward. Both programmes elicited a positive response from participants and their families, but there are no figures available to say whether or not there was a subsequent reduction in vendetta killings.[39]

For Remacka:

> The global education project played a key role in post-totalitarian democratic society in Albania by contributing to developing civil society. One of the most important impacts of the project was family involvement in schools by stressing the reciprocal partnership in order to maximise the educational process. In its progress, the global education mandate has reached a platform of official and school acceptance against the authoritarian, hierarchy, injustice and mediocrity approach through curricular, cross-curricular and extra-curricular (community) development.[40]

Endnote

This chapter has explored the community relevance and potential of a holistic, transformative model of global education and its attendant pedagogy using storied cases from three developing-world contexts. The model emanates from Western countries in the economically affluent North (the

United Kingdom and Canada) while the stories are ones about cross-cultural partnerships for change between a university centre in Canada, on the one hand, and a varied mix of government and municipal organisations, businesses and (international and national) not-for-profit organisations based in developing nations, on the other. The Canadian university centre provided the initial conceptual framing for each partnership project and undertook a consultancy, facilitation and capacity-building role of initial but progressively diminishing prominence. Dialogue between the partners but, increasingly, in-country action and dialogue as capacity and experience accumulated, led to each application of global education becoming distinctive, even unique. Local communities and activists have played a signal part in this latter process. In this way a global dialogue on the nature, purposes and processes of global education has been built so that the model itself, as all models should be, comes to be more clearly perceived as a living 'in-process' affair, subject to revision, however small, with every touch on the web of connections.

* * *

References

1. L. Sauvé (1999) 'Environmental Education Between Modernity and Postmodernity: Searching for an Integrating Educational Framework', *Canadian Journal of Environmental Education* Vol. 4, Summer 1999, p.19.

2. D. Selby (2005) 'Responding to Globalisation and the Global Condition: Technocratic Skills or Normative Ideals for Transformation? A Critique of Douglas Bourn's Conception of Global Education', *Zeitschrift für internationale Bildungsforschung und Entwicklungspädagogik* (Journal for International Education Research and Development Education) Vol. 28 No. 1, p.37.

3. See, for instance, Department for Education and Skills (2004) *Putting the World into World-class Education: An international strategy for education, skills and children's services*, Department for Education and Skills; also, D. Bourn (2005) '"Interconnectedness versus Interdependence": Reflections in response to David Selby', *Zeitschrift für internationale Bildungsforschung und Entwicklungspädagogik* Vol. 28 No. 1, pp.29-34.

4. T. Swee-Hin (1993) 'Bringing the World into the Classroom: Global Literacy and a Question of Paradigms', *Global Education* (Alberta Global Education Project) Vol. 1 No.1, January 1993, pp.10-11.

5. *Ibid.* p.11.

6. D. Selby (2007) 'As the Heating Happens: Education for Sustainable Development or Education for Sustainable Contraction', *International Journal of Innovation and Sustainable Development* Vol. 2 Nos. 3/4, pp.259-9.

7. D. Selby (2000) 'Global Education as Transformative Education', *Zeitschrift für internationale Bildungsforschung und Entwicklungspädagogik*, Vol. 28 No.3, pp.2-10.

See, also, T. Swee-Hin, *op.cit.*

8. P. Teller (1986) 'Relational Holism and Quantum Mechanics', *British Journal for the Philosophy of Science* Vol 37, pp.71-81.

9. For a fuller exposition of the four-dimensional model, see: G. Pike & D. Selby (1999/2000) *In the Global Classroom, Book 1* and *Book 2*, Pippin Publishing, Toronto.

10. For a discussion of global education learning processes arising from the model, see: G. Pike & D. Selby (1999) *Global Education: Making Basic Learning a Child-friendly Experience*, UNICEF, Amman. Also D. Selby (2000) 'Global Education as Transformative Education', *Zeitschrift für internationale Bildungsforschung und Entwicklungspädagogik* Vol. 28 No.3.

11. See, for instance, G. Pike & D.Selby (1999/2000) *Global Teacher, Global Learner*, Hodder & Stoughton, 1988; G. Pike & D. Selby, *In the Global Classroom. Book 1* and *Book 2*, Pippin Publishing, Toronto.

12. For NIEGA visit [accessed 19 June 2008].

13. M. Santos (2004) *Discovering New Paths for Global Citizenship Education in Brazil: Three Case Studies*. MA thesis, Department of Curriculum, Teaching and Learning, Ontario Institute for Studies in Education of the University of Toronto, p.128.

14. *Ibid.*

15. *Ibid.*, p.131.

16. *Ibid.*, p.133.

17. For a full account of the social housing agency developments (from which the data offered here is taken), see *Ibid.* 135-140. See, also, NIEGA, *Global Education: A Reference for Environmental Training in Different Organisational Contexts,* NIEGA, São Paulo, mimeo, pp.2-7.

18. *Ibid.*, p.145.

19. *Ibid.*, p.144.

20. *Ibid.*, p.143-4. For a full account of the 'Save our Sea' story (from which the data offered here is taken), see *Ibid.*, p.141-7.

21. *Ibid.*, p.214.

22. *Ibid.*, p.215.

23. For 'Woolly Thinking,' see G. Pike & D.Selby (1988) *Global Teacher, Global Learner*, Hodder & Stoughton, p.141.

24. M. Santos (2004) *Discovering New Paths for Global Citizenship Education in Brazil: Three Case Studies*. MA thesis, Department of Curriculum, Teaching and Learning, Ontario Institute for Studies in Education of the University of Toronto, pp.218-21.

25. *Ibid.*, pp.222-3. For a full account of Project Polis (from which the data offered here is taken), see *Ibid.*, pp.210-223.

26. G. Pike & D. Selby (1999) *Global Education: Making Basic Learning a Child-friendly Experience*, UNICEF, Amman, 1-2, pp.29-46.

27. For the various UNICEF initiatives referred to, other than Albania (for which see endnote 41 below) see: R.G. Sultana (2000) *The Global Education Initiative: Syria's Flying Carpet*, UNICEF, Amman; M. Mahdavinia (2006) *An Evaluative Case Study*

of UNICEF *Global Edcation Project in Iran, 2000-2003,* doctoral thesis, Department of Curriculum, Teaching and Learning, Ontario Institute for Studies in Education of the University of Toronto (for summary); Souykhudyan (2000) *Life Skills Education in Armenia,* paper presented at The Future of Our Children Education for Peace International Meeting, University of Geneva, 4-8 September 2000. For a description of the UNICEF CARK Global Education Initiative, go to:

28. G. Pike & D. Selby (1999), *Global Education: Making Basic Learning a Child-friendly Experience,* UNICEF, Amman, p.30.

29. *Ibid.,* p.112.

30. *Ibid.,* p.113.

31. *Ibid.,* p.115.

32. *Ibid.,* p.114.

33. *Ibid.,* pp.117-8.

34. *Ibid.,* p.114.

35. For the full story of the Lebanese Global Education Initiative, see *Ibid.* pp.29-32, pp.39-44, pp.111-127.

36. C. Ashton (2000) *Global Education Project: Evaluation Report for Second Phase,* Ministry of Education and Science Albania/Institute of Pedagogical Studies/UNICEF/International Institute for Global Education, University of Toronto, Tirana, Albania, November 2000, pp.38-9; D. Selby (2000) *Global Education in Albania Project: Mission Report, 6-12 September 2000,* UNICEF, mimeo, p.7.

37. L. Remacka, *GE Project in Albania,* personal communication, dated 22 June 2008, p.1.

38. *Ibid.,* p.2.

39. D. Selby, *Global Education in Albania Project: Mission Report, 6-12 September 2000,* UNICEF, mimeo, p.6.

40. L. Remacka, *GE Project in Albania,* personal communication, dated 22 June 2008, p.2.

41. *Ibid.,* p.1. For narrative and evaluative accounts of the Global Education Project in Albania, see: A. Dautaj, F. Myteberi, M. Gjokutaj & S. Llambiri (2000) *Global Education Project: Report on Phase One Evaluation,* UNICEF, Tirana; D.Selby, G. Pike, F. Myteberi, S. Llambiri, A. Dautaj, B. Rexha (2000) *Global Education: Preparation of Children to Face Up to Challenges of 21st Century. Teacher Manual for Global Education,* UNICEF, Tirana; C. Ashton (2000) *Global Education Project: Evaluation Report for Second Phase,* Ministry of Education and Science Albania/Institute of Pedagogical Studies/UNICEF/International Institute for Global Education, University of Toronto, Tirana, Albania, November 2000; L. Remacka (2002) *Global Citizenship Education in Albania,* M. Ed, Major Research Paper, Department of Curriculum, Teaching and Learning, Ontario Institute for Studies in Education of the University of Toronto.

Chapter Four

Empowerment through education: SCAD's experience

by Dr S. Cletus Babu

Introduction

Social Change And Development (SCAD) believes that education is the first step towards empowerment. SCAD adopts formal and non-formal education programmes to awaken the people to taste the fruits of empowerment in the southern Districts of Tamil Nadu in south India. SCAD works in three backward and drought-prone districts, namely Tirunelveli, Tuticorin and Kanyakumari Districts by reaching out to nearly 200,000 people in 453 rural villages. Since its inception in 1985, SCAD has been empowering the most marginalised groups including women, landless agricultural labourers, small and marginal farmers, uneducated and unemployed youth, physically and mentally challenged children, saltpan workers, gypsies, snake charmers, leprosy patients, palmyrah tappers and quarry workers. SCAD primarily works in the spheres of education, health, community organisation and Integrated Rural Development initiatives.

Socio-educational status in the target area

The people targeted by SCAD are socially weak and economically poor. They are ignorant and illiterate, which allows various forces to exploit them in every way.

The illiteracy is very high: 63% among the *dalits*,[1] gypsies, leprosy-affected, saltpan workers, landless labourers and fisher-people. Poverty perpetuates illiteracy, which in turn perpetuates ignorance and exploitation among the poverty-stricken. In most of the target communities of SCAD, child labour is predominant and SCAD makes a deliberate intervention to promote education and literacy.

A mass literacy movement is needed to educate and to awaken the people, and SCAD is much involved in this field through its people-centred development initiatives. SCAD firmly believes that no development is possible without education. Hence it works hard to engender change by making people leave the chauvinistic caste-based and exploitative education by educating and conscientising[2] them in the values of equality, justice and fraternity.

SCAD undertook its first initiatives in the year 1985, with the objective of educating the non-school-going village children and the uneducated adults in non-formal education centres. Over the years, its commitment and involvement in education has brought much acclaim and fame to SCAD within this part of southern India. How the liberating and change-oriented education of SCAD evolved from the earlier caste-based and conservative education is the subject of this chapter. As founder and the Managing Director of SCAD, I am very pleased to share this developmental experience with readers of this book.

Caste-based education of the past

In the past, education was the reserve of high-caste people in India. The *Varnashramadharma*[3] quotes that the Brahmanical caste (superior castes in the caste hierarchy) are entitled to get education and to learn *vedasastra*,[4] whereas the other lower castes are destined to serve the high castes by remaining submissive to them. Some castes belonging to the lowest rung in the caste hierarchy are literally considered as 'untouchables' in all walks of life.

Primary and basic education was denied to the backward castes, scheduled castes (*dalits*) and scheduled tribes even in the Government administered schools and colleges before Independence in 1947. The high-caste students enjoyed the privileges of sitting on the chairs and benches in the schools, whereas the so-called low-caste students sat separately on the floor and were treated very badly by the teachers, who were mostly from high castes.

This caste-based, chauvinistic and oppressive education was abolished by the Indian Constitution after Independence, and all the citizens of India are now entitled to rights and privileges irrespective of caste, creed and ethnic affinity. The Constitution is based on the egalitarian principles of equality, justice and fraternity. However, even after Independence, the conservative forces continued to promote caste-based discrimination within education wherever possible. Even today, the discrimination and atrocities against Harijans[5] and backward castes in the schools, villages, public places, hotels, etc. can be witnessed sporadically despite the bad publicity in the media.

In this context, SCAD took an ethical and altruistic stand by serving the most marginalised and most oppressed people in the society.

Non-formal education methods of SCAD

SCAD started working in the villages of Tirunelveli District in 1980s with a bunch of committed and dedicated people selected from the communities. It concentrated in the very backward areas of Cheranmahadevi in Tirunelveli District by working with twenty villages. Later, SCAD also worked in Tuticorin District as well. The SCAD staff used non-formal education as an entry point to make an intervention in the morning and evening hours, teaching people the basic alphabet and awareness-raising songs to develop interest in the non-formal education centres and activities SCAD was promoting. In time, the sincere and committed work of SCAD community organisers won the hearts of the village people, who started sending their children to the SCAD non-formal education centres regularly. The gradual increase in the number of the children attending these classes made SCAD rethink its old strategy and adopt a new one of enrolling more and more children in formal schools.

Enrolment campaigns of SCAD

SCAD could make its presence felt in hundreds of its working villages by concentrating on the non-school-going children. The SCAD volunteers and activists decided to conduct enrolment campaigns in all the working villages. To this end, SCAD started conducting enrolment campaigns by organising the children and conducting a door-to-door campaign in the villages to insist the parents should enrol their own children in the schools. The slogans taught to the women's self-help group members included:

"No to work, yes to education", "Let us enrol all the children above five years in schools" and "Let us abolish child labour from our families and the village". These kindled in the minds of the parents the belief that their children ought to receive formal education.

SCAD made up its mind to conduct enrolment campaigns in all the working villages after witnessing the rewarding results of the campaigns.

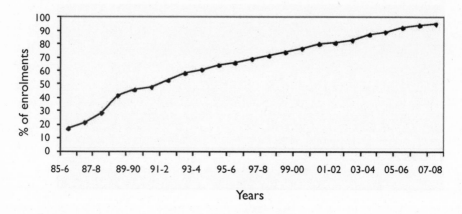

Table 4.1: School enrolments

The gradual and steady increase in the enrolment of children made SCAD concentrate on providing quality and child-centred education to all children. The diagram above indicates the gradual growth in the enrolment of children in schools in SCAD target blocks.

Promotion of child-centred education in schools

SCAD started collaborating with the government and privately administered primary schools in early 1990s in the blocks of Tirunelveli, Tuticorin, Vilathikulam, Ottapidaram and Tiruchendur. Much emphasis was given to child-centred education, and the gaps and challenges in imparting child-centred education were addressed and rectified by SCAD with timely and need-based interventions. These included:

Appointing educated unemployed as teachers in the schools

SCAD found out that lack of sufficient teachers in the village-based primary schools led to a deterioration in the standard of education among school-going children. Hence, in collaboration with the individual school managements, SCAD appointed volunteers who had proper education as teachers in those schools where existing staffing level was just one or two. The volunteers have been trained in child-centred teaching and play methods. This has improved the educational attainments of children, making many of them shine often on a par with the more advantaged children studying in advanced schools, whose parents have to pay very high fees. The honoraria for the volunteers are paid by SCAD.

Besides educating the children, the volunteers play a dynamic role in animating the parents to participate in the Parent Teachers Association (PTA) meetings and to work for the general improvement of the educational level and standard in the villages.

Provision of infrastructural facilities in the village schools

Almost all the schools in the remote and backward villages of the SCAD target blocks lack basic infrastructural facilities such as spacious classrooms, furniture, toilets/urinals, educative materials, play equipments/materials etc. Having realised the importance of infrastructural facilities in quality education, SCAD itself provides many of the above materials by encouraging people to contribute something in all its initiatives.

S.No	Category	Number of Schools
1	Construction of classrooms	136
2	Repair and renovation of school buildings	172
3	Provision of furniture (tables/benches)	215
4	Construction of toilets/urinal blocks	63
5	Educative materials (charts/globes/books etc.)	348
6	Play equipment (jungle gym, seesaws, swings etc.)	397
7	Play materials (balls, rings, bats etc.)	443

Table 4.2: SCAD's assistance in providing infrastructural facilities in schools.

Activating the Village Education Committees

SCAD forms village education committees with the participation of the local villagers drawn from various walks of life. Equal representation is given to both men and women in all the education committees. The committees convene meetings once in a month, and discuss the various issues and challenges which affect the schools in delivering quality education to children. The committee members collectively find solutions to these challenges and problems. They are the main activists mobilising support for the schools from within the village communities and so constantly improving its work and service. SCAD volunteers and the people's organisations play a proactive role in the Village Education Committees.

Promotion of various student associations and forums

SCAD believes that preschool and primary school education is very important in developing them as future responsible adults and citizens of India. The following clubs have been promoted in the Schools by SCAD volunteers:

- The Environmental and Eco Club
- Kutty Doctors Club
- Self-Employment Club
- Cultural Activities Promotion Club

The student representatives from class three to five are the active members of the club. The club members create a chance and opportunities to exhibit their innate talents and to awaken many ideas in their peers, parents and the village people. The Environmental and Eco club members are involved in planting trees, maintaining school gardens, safely disposing of rubbish, separating the plastic from the perishable waste and so encouraging village people to become more environmentally friendly. The Kutty doctors club involves fully ensuring personal and environmental hygiene. They start their activities by educating each and every student in the school on matters of personal hygiene like bathing, brushing teeth, washing clothes, keeping the house and its surroundings clean and hygienic, disseminating information on first aid and dispensing herbal medicines for day-to-day ailments, etc. The students who belong to the Self-Employment Club learn knitting, wire bag making, basket weaving, mat weaving and making ornamental and decorative items from waste materials. They also teach other students to learn these self-employment skills. The students belonging to the Cultural Activities Promotion Club regularly organise Tamil Association forum meetings in the school, motivating and facilitating the students to exhibit their innate talents and skills.

There are 450 fully operational schools supported by SCAD. They are clearly making a real change in the lives and minds of the village children.

Evening tuition for the slow learners

Once the slow learners in the village schools have been identified, special care and attention is given to ensure they can study in similar ways to other children. SCAD's 'barefoot teachers' enable them to learn the subjects through the play-based method of teaching. The SCAD evening tuition centres not only focus on education but also on the real life issues affecting the communities. The Village Development Councils, the men's and women's Self-Help Groups and other user groups make use of the centres after 8pm to discuss and to find solutions to their day-to-day problems.

Enabling village children to complete their schooling

SCAD ensures all village children get a primary education. Unfortunately not all the village schools have facilities for secondary and higher secondary education. Hence the SCAD volunteer and the village education committees regularly follow up on each child to get them admitted to nearby secondary and higher secondary schools.

When a volunteer finds children from poverty-stricken families having difficulties paying for their education, they recommend the child gets further help. SCAD does the needs assessment with the help of its staff, and aids these poor children to complete their schooling by increasing the necessary financial assistance. In the evening, SCAD volunteers offer all possible help to adolescent boys or girls to understand the difficult subjects, especially Maths, Science and English, and to help them score good marks in the exams. More than thirty thousand students are helped in this way. SCAD helps those students who are unable to pursue their education by becoming day-scholars by enrolling them in the nearby hostels run by both government and private providers. SCAD therefore supports the poor and disadvantaged children in many ways to achieve well during their education.

The need for vocational skill training and employment-oriented education

Every year thousands of students come from schools after completing their higher secondary education without having any goal or focus in life. More than 60% of rural students cannot compete with the more advantaged students who get educated in advanced schools, so they opt for any college degree which ultimately makes them educated but sometimes unemployed too. Having realised the problems of the educated unemployed in the villages, SCAD started providing employment-oriented skills and vocational education in many fields.

Creating opportunities for students to do higher education

In many districts SCAD has created viable opportunities for students to access higher education in technical institutions. These institutions have been established by SCAD, and deliver quality skill and technical training to very needy students from very backward rural communities. They include:

Francis Xavier Engineering College

Francis Xavier Engineering College is situated in Tirunelveli, the district headquarters. This college has been functioning since 2000 with a motto "Development through technology", and offers the following excellent courses:

- B.E. Computer Science and Engineering
- B.E. Electronics and Communication Engineering
- B.E. Electrical and Electronics Engineering
- B.E. Mechanical Engineering
- B.Tech. Information Technology
- M.E. Computer Science and Engineering
- M.E. VLSI
- M. Tech. Information Technology
- M.B.A.
- M.C.A.

Francis Xavier Engineering College offers special merit-based scholarships to poor students, with a special emphasis on the poorest of the poor – students belonging to the scheduled caste, scheduled tribes, most backward and backward castes. The College gives preferential options for the students from poverty-stricken families in the SCAD rural working villages.

A minimum of 60 to a maximum of 90 students study on each course. In total, 75% or more students are from the families of very deserving communities. There are special seminars, debates, workshops, placement trainings, in-plant training, industrial visits, personality development, career guidance programmes, real-time projects, paper presentations, advanced computer labs, well-equipped library and laboratory facilities, co-curricular and extra-curricular activities offered in the college, enabling the students to excel in many areas of learning, creative thinking and doing.

SCAD College of Engineering and Technology
SCAD College of Engineering and Technology has been offering development and technological courses with a team of committed and excellent teaching faculty. The following courses are being offered in the college:

- B.E. Computer Science and Engineering
- B.E. Electronics and Communication Engineering
- B.E. Electrical and Electronics Engineering
- B.E. Mechanical Engineering
- B.Tech. Information Technology
- M.E. Computer Science and Engineering
- M.E. Network
- M.B.A.
- M.C.A.

Like the other SCAD institutions, this leading college offers help for meritorious students from the disadvantaged communities and empowers them to be future change agents wherever they live and work.

SCAD Polytechnic College
SCAD Polytechnic College has been imparting value-based technical education for the betterment of socially and economically backward sections of society since 1997. The vision of this institute is to ensure quality education by adopting better standards and procedures. Diploma courses offered in the college include Mechanical, Electrical, Civil and Computer Engineering as well as Information and Print Technology. Students taking these courses have very good employment prospects.

Francis Xavier Polytechnic College
Francis Xavier Polytechnic College was established in 2006 at Tharuvai near Tirunelveli, with the principal objective of bringing quality education within the reach of students particularly from the rural areas. Since its ori-

gin, this College has been imparting professional technical education with an emphasis on analytical and reasoning abilities as well as practical skills.

SCAD Industrial Technical Institutes

SCAD has been administering two industrial technical institutes, one at Cheranmahadevi in Tirunelveli District and another at Vagaikulam in Tuticorin district. The six-monthly courses on motor mechanics, electrical wiring, fitter and diesel mechanics are being studied by 80 youths in each institute. These young people from poor rural areas have failed their tenth standard exam but are given preference in the institutes' admission systems. The technical courses and the holistic education imparted to the students equip them to bravely face the many challenges in life.

SCAD Teacher Training Institute

The SCAD Teacher Training Institute is situated at the SCAD Campus Cheranmahadevi, and it has been educating 50 very deserving candidates from the rural villages every year. It has committed and inspired teachers. Besides the regular curriculum, a thorough exposure to social and development dynamics is given to teacher trainees as a way of making them exemplary teachers in the future.

SCAD College of Education

The college of education at SCAD Campus Cheranmahadevi aims to train dynamic young men and women to become illustrious and committed teachers. A total of 100 students are trained here every year. The young men and women who leave this college every year shine in their careers because of the input they experienced during their training. Like with other institutions, SCAD adopts an altruistic policy of admitting the most deserving and poor students from the rural areas to this college.

SCAD Community College

The Community College in SCAD Campus Cheranmahadevi aims to deliver job-oriented courses for the poor rural boys and girls who have completed their higher secondary exams. The courses on Computer Science, Nursing, Motor Mechanics and Air Conditioning are offered to 200 candidates from the disadvantaged communities. These students are trained for a period of one year and join different employers, often with a good salary, as soon as they complete their studies.

SCAD Nutrition School and nutrition biscuit-manufacturing unit

SCAD also runs a Nutrition School and nutrition biscuit-manufacturing unit at Cheranmahadevi. This unit produces four lakh[6] biscuits every year and the same are distributed to 1,000 malnourished children in the working villages. These nutritious biscuits are being produced by adding cowpea extract, which is rich in Vitamin A (Beta-Carotene). Education on nutrition is delivered by a team headed by a home scientist. Low-cost nutritive food items are used in the demonstrations which help teach people the value of improved nutritive practices and better health.

SCAD Anbu illam Special Schools for the physically and mentally challenged

SCAD administers a special school exclusively for the physically and mentally challenged. This special school has been in action since 2001. To begin with only 12 children were helped, but now it serves 97 children suffering from mental retardation, autism, cerebral palsy and various categories of learning difficulty including mild, moderate, severe and profound.

Two special educators, two teaching assistants, two physiotherapists and one assistant therapist look after and educate the children with enthusiasm and total commitment. Sensory integration therapy, speech therapy, physiotherapy and occupational therapy are given to the children to improve their physical and mental well-being.

SCAD runs a special school for the physically challenged on the SCAD campus. A total of 257 children have so far benefited from the school. At present 69 children are studying there. Various types of disabilities including speech, hearing and sight impairment and other forms of physical disability are given special treatment, care, medication, physiotherapy, exercise and training to improve their well-being. Children who could undergo operations and partially or fully recover from their disabilities are sent for treatment in well-furnished government and private hospitals.

SCAD empowerment programmes for uneducated rural women

SCAD organises the training of uneducated rural women in grassroots organisations and educates them in various empowerment initiatives. 2,500 Self-Help Groups have been formed in 453 remote and backward villages to stimulate and sustain change in socio-economic, cultural and political areas of life. The empowerment and solidarity women develop through education makes this possible. The non-formal education and capacity-building programmes delivered to women create change in every sphere of life. These include:

Formation of people's organisations

The people's organisations formed at the grassroots level in the villages have over the years done much to address the oppression of women, young girls, scheduled castes and backward caste families. SCAD frames a curriculum for education and training as capacity-building programmes which are delivered to the people at regular intervals.

Training on group formation and savings

Training on group formation stimulates women to think about the need to form women's groups and federations. It clearly teaches them the benefits of group formation and the nature of group dynamics. The basic philosophy of women's groups, the principles on which they are built, the gender issues and sensitisation to gender needs and problems, are the discussion points in the training programmes. Additionally, the training programmes inculcate in them the habit of financial saving, credit management, book keeping and accounts maintenance. The women greatly benefit from this, and many women in the villages have developed real leadership skills and capabilities.

Training in entrepreneurial skills and income generation

SCAD organises ten entrepreneurial training programmes every month for a minimum of 300 to a maximum of 500 women. These women are shown the way to secure bank loans at minimum interest rates, and to start their own entrepreneurial initiatives or income-generation pro-grammes. Hundreds of women are now successful entrepreneurs, setting good examples to others.

SCAD has a number of successful women entrepreneurs with multifac-eted entrepreneurial skills and abilities including horticultural nursery production, making simple chemicals, vermi-compost making, mushroom production, running dairy co-operatives, managing small shops, making rexin bags and ready-made garment production. Besides these initiatives, the SCAD women's Self-Help Groups are capable of administering various other income-generation programmes specific to their local conditions.

Occupational employment programmes for small and marginal farmers, fisher-people and palmyra tree tappers

India generally and the Districts SCAD targets in particular has more than 70% of the people dependent on agriculture for their sustenance. More than 80% of the SCAD target blocks depend on the north-east monsoon rains for their agricultural activities. Only 20% of the target blocks benefit from assured irrigation from the Tamiraparani river. Hence SCAD promotes sustainable agricultural programmes for the small and marginal farmers. Old practices are being taught such as farm pond making, bio-pesticide making, bio-compost making and vermi-composting, inter-cropping, pest control and management, reviving the traditional drought-resistant seeds, etc. Demonstrations of farm assessment methods are given to local farmers so as to reduce farm expenses and improve farm production.

The farmers are made aware of multinational companies which promote mono-cropping and terminator seeds which put the very lives and livelihoods of farmers in danger. SCAD subject specialists and farm scientists educate the farmers in the tried and tested methods in the SCAD Farm Science Centre, giving them the additional input and training on fish farming, bee keeping, milch animal rearing, goat, pig and poultry rearing. This enables them to invest their resources in different areas of activity to earn sustainable and better incomes. The farmers whose livelihoods rely on palm-tree tapping are given training on value-added activities so as to secure a better income from palm-tree juice, leaves, fruits and other byproducts. This timely training has also helped them to form co-operatives. More than 5,000 families of palm tree tappers have been helped in this manner.

More than 5,000 small country boat fisher-people are organised and federated by SCAD to free themselves from the clutches of moneylenders, middle men and from the vices of drinking and gambling. The fisher-people federations are helped through constant training programmes and a revolving fund. Conscientisation within the training programmes encourages critical thinking and broad environmental awareness.

Other skills training programmes

SCAD informally administers various other skill-training programmes. These programmes help the semi-skilled and skilled and uneducated women and men to find a way to escape the persistent problems of poverty. SCAD financially supports training in office skills, computer programming, electrical trades, plumbing, cycle repairing, candle- and incense-stick-making, fishnet weaving, horticulture and other activities. SCAD also runs twelve mobile tailoring units, each with a skilled teacher, an assistant and all the necessary machinery and equipment. These mobile units deliver six-monthly training programmes in the remote villages, and train adolescent boys and girls in the skills of cutting and stitching. 1,766 people have so far been trained, and 80% of them are employed in the ready-made garment-making units in and outside Tuticorin and Tirunelveli districts. Another 7% are running their own successful units. SCAD administers four Rexin bag-making units which gives training to 77 women and men. The trained women are shown how to secure bank loans and run their own Rexin bag-making units. The orders from schools and other educational institutions enable the units to run profitably. And finally, SCAD operates three mech-anised boat repairing units and two outboard machine repairing units in the coastal villages of Tuticorin and Tirunelveli Districts. A total of 227 young fisher-people benefit from these units.

The impact of the SCAD educational development programme

The difference SCAD makes in the lives of marginalised people through education is clearly evident:

- Primary education: SCAD delivers child-centred education even in the remote villages of Tirunelveli and Tuticorin Districts, and is changing the lives of approximately 50,000 marginalised children.

- The empowerment education programme gives employment and livelihood opportunities for more than a thousand people. The educational service and standards of village schools have been improved. Many students, particularly girls, have benefited.

- The infrastructural facilities such as spacious classrooms, furniture, toilets/urinals, educative materials and play equipment have been improved, making for more conducive learning environments in the village schools.

- Formation and active functioning of the village education committees made a sea change in more than 1,000 rural villages which would otherwise remain severely disadvantaged and deprived.

- The forming of students' associations/forums and four basic clubs have made the children responsible for their own and their village's development. This approach helps children to develop a broader approach and thinking, nurturing social responsibility from an early age.

- Special concentration is given to slow learners, enabling them to study well and to succeed. Thousands of children from the backward villages have benefited.

- General assistance to 30,000 students in secondary and higher secondary education has enabled them to complete their schooling.

- SCAD's assistance in higher education has changed the lives of many individuals, families, communities and society at large. Thousands of young people have been made aware of sustainable development.

- SCAD's highly valued educational and technical institutions educate thousands of impoverished students every year. They are continuously serving disadvantaged people.

- Many poor women in rural areas have been organised in community groups and federated at a village-based panchayat, block, district level and regional level for greater conscientisation and practical action.

- The continuous training programmes for village women enhance their thinking and improve their knowledge on various subjects ranging from financial saving to entrepreneurial initiatives. They ultimately become change agents in their villages.

- Many successful entrepreneurs and income generators emerge from village communities, and they show the way to others by being successful.

- In the light of globalisation and its repercussions, SCAD ensures occupational employment programmes for thousands of small and marginal farmers, fisher-people and palmyra-tree tappers in schemes promoting integrated and sustainable development.

Conclusion

In India only 20% of the people get an opportunity for higher and technical education. SCAD aims to increase the numbers of students going to higher education by making more opportunities available. SCAD has a committed team and a well-equipped Vocational Skill Training Centre to help rural people with both life skills and developmental skills. SCAD promotes integrated sustainable development, reaching out to the small and marginal farmers, fisher-people, gypsies, leprosy-affected, snake catchers, Palmyra-tree tappers, saltpan workers and to the very poorest sections in society. SCAD plans to intensify both formal and non-formal educational interventions, and to empower the poor rural people by addressing the very important issues of low wages, unsustainable agricultural practices, exploitative money-making and gender issues. We are very interested in collaborating with funding partners who agree with our thinking, and we are confident of creating positive change both in the minds and lives of disadvantaged and marginalised people. SCAD is open to new ideas and new people–centred development programmes. SCAD's experience in empowering people through education is possibly a model for others. We believe that change is only possible through value-based development education. Let us all unite and empower the poor through change-oriented education, and create a world where the values of justice, equality and fraternity dominate.

* * *

References
P. Freire (1972) *Pedagogy of the Oppressed*, Penguin, Harmondsworth.

Website
SCAD website: www.scadindia.org.

Notes
1. '*Dalit*' – members of the lowest caste, formerly known as 'untouchables'.
2. A term derived from the work of the radical educator Paulo Freire, who in his *Pedagogy of the Oppressed* (1972) refers to 'conscientisation' as the process by which men and women actively achieve a deepening awareness of the socio-cultural reality that shapes their lives and of their capacity to transform that reality.
3. *Varnashramadharma*: a code for living for members of Hindu caste society.
4. A sacred Hindu text.

A brief explanation of the Indian caste system

According to Manusmriti, the ancient Hindu Scriptures, there are four categories of castes namely Brahmanas, Kshatriyas, Vaisias and Shudras. The ancient Hindu scriptures say that Brahmanas are the highest people in the caste order originating from the head of 'Brahma', the God of creation. The head is associated with Knowledge, Power and Wisdom and so these people are destined to rule and to administer priestly duties.

The Kshatriyas are the second in the caste hierarchy originating from the chest of 'Brahma'. The chest is associated with valour, courage and confidence and so these people are destined to protect the country and the people from enemies and natural disaster. People from this category are mostly kings and warriors; in short, the rulers of the country or region.

The Vaisias are the third in the caste hierarchy originating from the stomach of the 'Brahma'. The stomach is associated with giving strength and sustenance to the whole body and hence these people are destined to toil, sweat and produce food and other things to fulfil the needs of people in society.

The Shudras are the fourth in the caste hierarchy originating from the feet of the 'Brahma'. The feet are associated with carrying the whole body. So these people are created just to serve the other three superior castes and their well-being by being peasants, traders and doing all other similar work. There are people who live outside the caste hierarchy and these are known to be 'untouchables' and 'the meanest beings' whose prime duties are doing the meanest things which the other so-called 'Caste Hindus' cannot do, i.e. cremating the dead, washing, cleaning the dead, cleaning and carrying human excreta, cleaning dead animals, clearing away sewage, and so on.

The scheduled caste, in other words '*dalits*', and the scheduled tribes (tribals), lead lives separate from mainstream society belong to the 'untouchables'. Hence the Indian government and the right-minded voluntary organisations work for the integrated development of these sections. But we need to go much further to eradicate the caste system and its heinous practices from the minds and lives of the people.

The Manudharma (Manu's principles) says if one person is born to a particular caste, he/she should faithfully carry out the duties and responsibilities of that caste, then he/she will be rewarded when reincarnated. Hinduism believes in seven births and finally a person can attain 'moksha' – the eternal bliss based on the 'karma' (action) of his/her existence. This is how caste divisions are justified, and people forced to accept their fate. Whether Christian or Muslim or any religion, everyone is placed into a particular caste at birth depending on the caste to which their parents belong.

The four broader categories of caste have produced innumerable other castes and sub-castes, and today there are about 1,000 castes and sub-castes. These are all recorded in the *Indian Gazette*.

5. Mahatma Gandhi called the scheduled castes 'Harijans', which means the Children of God.

6. A 'lakh' is a unit in the Indian numbering system equal to 100,000.

Chapter Five

Economic and social development of fisher-people through the work of Village Development Councils (VDCs): SCAD's experience

by G. Nagarajan

Introduction

The state of Tamil Nadu in southern India has a coastline of 435 kilometres, and nearly ten million people depend on fishing and other marine resources for their sustenance. The Districts of Tirunelveli and Tuticorin, targeted by the grassroots non-governmental organisation (NGO) known as Social Change and Development (SCAD), also have a long coastline (235 kilometres), and millions of people depend on sea for their sustenance.

Socio-economic conditions of the fisher-people in South Tamil Nadu

The fisher-people in south Tamil Nadu belong to different faiths, namely Hinduism, Christianity and Islam. This division can also be seen among the fisher-people. The mechanised boat owners are considered to be the richest, the country boat owners are considered to be the middle income group, and the small fish merchants who carry the fish baskets on their heads and are involved in the sale of fish are considered to be the poorest income group. In most of the fisher villages more than 75% of people belong to the poorest income group, 19% belong to the middle income group, and only 6% to the high and very high income group.

The income of the fisher-people is reflected in their living conditions too. The poor and marginal fisher-people live in thatched or asbestos-roofed houses with one room and a small kitchen. The middle income fisher-people live in tiled-roof houses with two or three rooms. The high and very high income fisher-people live in concrete houses with all the modern facilities such as televisions, refrigerators, air-conditioners, washing machines and other modern gadgets.

The squalid working conditions of the fisher-people affect their health too. The unhygienic working conditions and the coastal shores themselves are breeding grounds for many diseases. Mosquito-related diseases like malaria, dengue, and other viral infections are very common in the coastal villages. The poverty-stricken and low-income fisher-people suffer worst of all.

Access to higher education

Access to higher education is confined for male fisher-children from well-off families. The female children and other male children from very poor families study up to primary or middle school education. 78% of them drop out after middle school because of the poverty within the families. Only 6% of children from fisher families proceed to higher education, and these have relatively affluent backgrounds.

Lack of unity among the fisher-people

Fisher-people in this region are also divided by caste, creed and political affiliation. Hence the forces of exploitation are able to cheat people by reinforcing their social divisions, and this prevents them from uniting around a focused goal for their lives. As a result, although the fisher-people constitute 18% of the total population of the state, they do not have any political representation which could strongly put their case.

Lack of technical skills and qualifications among fisher youth

More than 83% of young people are involved in fishing and allied activities. Though the marine resources are depleting fast, young people have not been able to diversify their interests to include trades other than fishing due to their lack of knowledge and understanding of the broader issues. Therefore it is very difficult to find young people who come from the fishing communities who are skilled and technically qualified in engineering and other technical areas.

Consequently, SCAD has adopted an integrated approach aiming at the holistic development of the lives of these young fisher-people. SCAD believes that any change or development should emerge from people. Hence, it started its work by conscientising[1] the fisher-people and organising them in different people's organisations, namely men's groups, women's groups and youth groups, and federating these at village, panchayat,[2] block and District level for greater collective action. SCAD's work has now started to increase school enrolment of fisher-children, particularly girls, and has increased the percentage of young people opting for higher studies; more people's organisations have started to emerge from fishing communities, and more and more fisher-people are now educated and trained in business and enterprise.

Of course the onslaught of the tsunami in December 2004 in south-east Asia drastically changed the lives of the target fishing communities, and more than two-thirds of the people in these fisher communities became destitute overnight. They expected a great deal of help to lift them from their desperate plight. In response, Social Change And Development intervened swiftly and intensively to help meet the needs of the fisher-people who had lost their livelihoods in the tsunami. Literally hundreds of coastal villages were affected.

Tsunami relief and rehabilitation activities

Immediately after the tsunami SCAD commenced the much-needed relief and rehabilitation work in 117 coastal villages in Tirunelveli, Tuticorin and Kanyakumari districts. The relief activities included cleaning away the debris, recovering and cremating the dead, and renovating the damaged houses, providing food, water, shelter, medicines and other basic necessities for the victims.

Innumerable boats had been damaged by the tidal waves in Kanyakumari, Tirunelveli and Tuticorin districts and the people affected naturally approached the development organisations for help to get their boats repaired. Unfortunately the needs of the fisher communities outweighed the funds available. Nonetheless, Council members made house visits and assessed every situation. They reviewed the Panchayat records and prepared a list of the worst-affected families, which was then used by State and District government officials to inform their own interventions.

The tsunami traumatised many of the survivors. Immediately after the tsunami more than 80% of fishermen were reluctant to resume their fishing activities as a result of fear and depression. Many fisher-people, young and old, remained idle, and to deal with this the Village Development Councils approached SCAD to develop viable and alternative income-generating activities and education and training programmes including tailoring, Rexin bag-making, ready-made garment making, cycle repair, computer literacy, net weaving, driving, bookbinding, and goat and poultry rearing. The councils have since expanded the number and scope of these programmes, which benefit more and more people every year.

After the initial relief activities, SCAD started other rehabilitation and community development work for the most affected people. SCAD found multi-caste and multicultural fisher-people scattered in the villages who had lost their direction and meaning in life. These people did not have any common platform to discuss their problems and issues or to communicate their needs. There were various Self-Help Groups, but they could not share their ideas and experiences with others as each group had its own location, interests, meeting times and places. The SCAD social work team tried to solve this problem but failed to do so for some time. The experience of working with the fisher-people and non-fishing communities finally led to the formation of a people's forum where solutions to problems could be discussed. This democratic and people-centred development forum was called the Village Development Council (VDC). The VDC worked with villages to facilitate people's direct participation, from the initial planning to the implementation stages of the development programmes, to ensure real and long-lasting change in the villages.

The VDCs framed criteria for selecting the most deserving people based on family income, type of house (thatched, tiled or concrete), nature of employment (daily labourer, small fishermen, big fishermen, gravity of damage incurred, etc.). Having done this, the VDCs supervised the repair of 1,042 partially damaged houses and construction of more than 300 new houses. The Councils identified more than 10,000 fisher families who had lost their nets, and these were given new ones so they could resume their occupations.

The creation and functioning of the Village Development Councils

Two representatives from each of the women's, men's, young people's, fish workers' and agricultural groups formed a development council in each village. The Village Development Councils represent all people in the village, so there are many voices present to discuss gender issues, wages, fish prices, yields from their fields and other issues related to the non-fulfillment of basic amenities and other common concerns. The VDCs quite often take decisions based on consensus, but sometimes by voting, in order to plan, implement and to follow up on the development programmes for the benefit of all the people in the villages. One person is democratically elected as the president and two others as secretary and treasurer by the members of the VDC. The secretary of the VDC is vested with the power of convening the meetings, preparing agendas for the meetings, writing minutes, directing the treasurer to sanction money for developmental needs in consultation with the president, scrutinising the bills and accounts and settling issues and problems between the members of the VDC and leaders of the Self Help Groups. After defining the roles and responsibilities of the office-holder of the village development councils, SCAD trained and motivated them to become leaders in their respective communities.

The major functions and responsibilities of the Village Development Councils can be summarised as follows:

- The VDCs encompass representatives from various groups of people who, shedding off their caste, creed and class background, come together once a month to discuss the developmental issues of the village, plan and implement welfare and developmental programmes in collaboration with Government and non-Governmental institutions.

- The VDCs select the beneficiaries for each developmental activity in consultation with other members, to enable these people to improve their lives and livelihoods.

- The VDCs scrutinise the financial accounts of village Self-Help Groups, reporting and recommending new developments to the collaborating organisation. In the case of any misappropriation of funds, the VDCs act in collaboration with the leaders of the Self-Help Groups to rectify the problem legally and peacefully.

- The VDCs work hand-in-hand with local elected Panchayat representatives to implement village development initiatives.
- Twice a month, the secretary of each VDC convenes the meeting and takes appropriate decisions pertaining to village development needs.
- The members of the VDC articulate the needs and issues and try to solve problems collaboratively, cordially and co-operatively.

Since their formation, the VDCs have done a wonderful job, particularly in the aftermath of tsunami, in reaching out to and assisting those people most in need. The following social action programmes demonstrates the key role VDCs play in helping to meet people's basic needs and amenities.

Regular supply of potable water to the fisher villages

Many fishing villages were deprived of regularly assured potable water due to past neglect from local official bodies. The Village Development Councils of Uvari, Periathalai and Kooduthalai villages petitioned the officials many times to no avail. Consequently, the members of the Village Development Councils staged a road 'rook' (road blockade) in the state highways of Tiruchendur to Uvari and blocked vehicles using the road. Three hours of blockade brought the District Revenue Officer to the site and made him conduct a negotiation with the people's leaders. People poured out all their demands, particularly the need for getting potable water regularly even in remote fisher villages. On the firm assurance from the District Revenue Officer, the protestors called off their blockade. Now people have a good water supply.

Good link roads and bus facilities for the fisher villages

The networking and federation of grassroots groups through Village Development Councils increased their strength and numbers enabling them play a positive role in engendering significant change in the villages. As a result, many coastal villages including Annanagar, Singhithurai, Kombuthurai, Sithavinayakanpatti and Velidupatti started getting good link roads, bus facilities and other basic amenities.

Electricity and house deeds for the poor people

More than three hundred poor people belonging to fisher and *dalit*[3] communities in Vembar Village did not get the facilities of electricity and house *patta*[4] despite many reminders to relevant officials in the electricity and revenue departments. This matter was brought to the attention of the members in the co-ordination committee meetings and discussed in public meetings. Immediately after the fisher-day celebration, area officials were instructed to take swift action, with many people getting electricity and their patta.

Mobilising various benefits for the people

The people most frequently targeted for assistance are the aged, the physically challenged, daughters and sons of poor widows and people faced with crippling poverty. The VDCs have mobilised resources and benefits from various Government departments:

- 264 old people were helped to acquire the government's assistance for the elderly, including a monthly stipend of Rs. 400 for each person.

- 78 physically challenged people were helped to get a monthly stipend of Rs. 800 from the government and to receive their identity cards which are necessary to claim those benefits due to them.

- 33 poor widows were given guidance and subsequently received assistance of Rs. 50,000 each from the government after giving away their daughters and sons in marriage.

- 118 students belonging to the fisher and *dalit* communities could apply for scholarship assistance to the tune of Rs. 10,000 each from the Education Department for continuing their education.

The impact of the Village Development Councils

The impact the VDCs have had can be easily summarised. They have:

- United the village people of different castes, creeds and political affiliations under one umbrella and given them a focused vision for their future lives.

- Given people a chance to articulate their views, discuss issues and problems and helped them to find solutions.

- Strengthened the relationship between the fishing and non-fishing communities.

- Empowered people helping them gain the freedom to decide their own future courses of action.

- Provided a sense of ownership among many community members which has been nurtured by their direct involvement and commitment.

- Helped shattered families from both the fishing and non-fishing communities to recover from the tsunami.

- Enabled people to be the agents of change in their own villages instead of always expecting help and change to come from outside.

- Have instilled in people values of self-reliance.

Conclusions

The VDCs have promoted and in many ways implement integrated and sustainable development, improving the conditions of many poor people. As a result, the councils have grown in power, status and confidence, leading them now to address broader human-rights violations and issues related to women's oppression. They have been supported by the concerted efforts of many people.

SCAD initially found it difficult to convince women to participate in the Village Development Council meetings, but continuous support and encouragement from the SCAD team helped many women to overcome their fears, suspicions and inhibitions. Today there are many women leaders who take up the issues and problems affecting fisher communities. They play an exemplary role and are a model to others. Unfortunately resources do not always meet every need. However, one thing is clear: if people are given a chance to lead an initiative or programme, they soon learn to make effective decisions about their future destiny. Development organisations should therefore play an enabling role allowing the people to take steering and leading roles.

The methods used by the Village Development Councils have ushered in a new era of development in the coastal villages which were badly affected by the tsunami. SCAD has sown the seeds of change and development in the minds of many people who, by their energy and participation, have achieved great results. SCAD feels proud of having helped to empower so many people. We are confident that future measures will continue to bring improvement and hope to the lives of many communities in the region.

* * *

References
P. Freire (1972) *Pedagogy of the Oppressed*, Penguin, Harmondsworth.

Notes
1. A term derived from the work of the radical educator Paulo Freire who in his *Pedagogy of the Oppressed* (1972) refers to 'conscientisation' as the process by which men and women actively achieve a deepening awareness of the socio-cultural reality that shapes their lives and of their capacity to transform that reality.
2. 'Panchayat' literally means assembly (yat) of five (panch) wise and respected elders chosen and accepted by the community. Traditionally, these assemblies settled disputes between individuals and villages. The term today refers to a system of devolved governance derived from 73rd amendment to the Indian Constitution passed in 1992 giving powers and responsibilities to 'panchayats' in the States to prepare plans for economic development and social justice and for their implementation.
3. '*Dalit*' – members of the lowest caste, formerly known as 'untouchables'.
4. The Patta Pass Book or title deed allows the holder to legally register certain transactions such as sales, gifts, mortgages, exchanges and other settlements.

Chapter Six

Human well-being and the natural environment

by Donna Ladkin

"In a misty dawn at the centre of the world is the morning star, tending cattle at the other side of this fence. Several years away you can see smoke from a hogan where an old man is cooking breakfast. He has already been outside to pray, recognised the morning star and his relationship to it, as he stands at the centre of miracles." – Joy Harjo

"The world is not what I see, it is what I live through."
– Maurice Merleau-Ponty

In this chapter I offer an account of the link between human well-being and the natural environment. In doing so, I primarily draw from philosophic rather than the more usual psychological discourse. In particular I look to the work of two twentieth-century phenomenologists, the Frenchman Maurice Merleau-Ponty (1908-1961), and the German Martin Heidegger (1889-1976), whose ideas, I believe, can bring new insights into the relationship between human and natural worlds. More specifically, the way in which Merleau-Ponty worked with the nature of human embodiment will be explored in more detail, as will Heidegger's notion of dwelling. In the concluding parts of the chapter, these ideas will be applied to more practical human endeavours in considering ideas of re-inhabitation as explored by the American environmental writer Stephanie Mills.

My purpose in writing this chapter is to present ideas from these writers which I believe offer new vantage points from which to describe and explore the intertwining of human and more-than-human perspectives. This is grounded in the belief that they illuminate the vital connection between humans and the world we inhabit in ways which can breathe new oxygen into it – thus providing the impetus, and perhaps energy, to engage differently with questions of ecological sustainability and social justice.

Theory on its own, whether from a psychological or philosophical perspective, can be rather dry, and it certainly does not often foster emotional states conducive to breakthroughs in habits of being. In order to bring some of the ideas alive, the chapter includes stories, both my own and others', in order to illustrate some of the more abstract notions introduced.

Before turning to the first of such stories, I'd like to take a small step backwards to consider the very terminology of the chapter itself. Just what is meant by the term 'the natural environment'? In particular, what does naming the chapter 'Human well-being and the natural environment' imply about the nature of human beings and the extent to which they are 'natural'? Furthermore, in what ways does it position 'more-than-human' entities as separate from humans in a way that might in fact contribute to a lack of well-being on humans' part? It is therefore to a brief unpacking of the assumptions and connotations informing the language, 'human well-being' and the 'natural environment' that I now turn.

Human beings and the 'natural environment': What is natural, what is human?

Firstly, my concern with the term 'natural environment', particularly when it is juxtaposed against 'human' in the way it is often used, is that it implies that humans are not natural. Although I would agree that there are differences between human ways of being in the world, and 'rock', or 'elephant', or 'bacterial' ways of being in the world, I would argue that in their own ways, rocks, elephants, bacteria and humans are 'natural'; that is, they have developed from evolutionary, earth-bound processes. In fact, it could be argued that conceptualising 'humans' and 'the natural environment' as distinct in this way could itself contribute to the alienation many humans experience in their relationship with the 'more-than-human' world. Leading from this, one of the key constructs this chapter seeks to call into question is that of humans, and human well-being, existing outside of the 'natural world'.

Coming at the construction from an alternative position, the notion of 'the natural environment' can connote ideas of 'pristine nature': that is, nature that has somehow escaped the influence of human intentionality in any way. Such an area of landmass is no longer available on any part of the planet. There may be limited regions of deep underwater oceans which have not been affected by human activity, but even this seems rather optimistic. Indeed, in any categorical sense, the 'natural environment' is no longer 'natural', if 'natural' is taken to mean not impacted upon by humans. Any trek through the British countryside, although considered a venture into 'the natural environment' by most ramblers, is in fact a journey through a landscape moulded by agricultural use, planning restrictions and artefacts of changing fashions. Even the most 'natural' elements of life itself, the air we breathe and the rain that falls from the sky, inevitably carry humanly-created pollutants.

This is not intended as a tirade against human intervention in the 'natural' world. Instead, in questioning the very terminology we so often take for granted, I wish to highlight the interweaving of 'human' and 'more-than-human' interactions in every aspect of living on planet Earth. Throughout the chapter I shall employ the phrase 'more-than-human', a term offered by David Abram in his book *The Spell of the Sensuous*, when I wish to differentiate between human and 'other' beings or forces with which humans engage on a minute-by-minute basis. This terminology is chosen to reduce the extent to which humans, and our well-being, are seen as distinctive from the 'natural world'. It is also to emphasise the immediate, continuous contact and interaction that occurs between humans and the more-than-human world. Not only is human 'well-being' related to the 'natural environment', but actual human 'being' is completely dependent on the Earth. The chapter aims to construct an argument which supports the claim that really knowing the deep dependency we have on the more-than-human world, and cultivating an orientation of care and gratitude toward it may well be the foundation from which human well-being can be robustly created.

In order to explore that proposition, I begin with a story of my own engagement with the more-than-human world and recognition of my dependence on it, by introducing you to the place I think of as home.

A story, a starting point

I think of 'home' as a small agricultural community in northern Maine, a place called Caribou, twenty miles south of the Canadian border at the head of the Aroostook River. Although my family moved there when I was ten, I still think of Caribou as the place that formed me, a sentiment shared by my younger brother and sister. There were two aspects of living in northern Maine which are particularly relevant to this chapter. Firstly,

Caribou was an agricultural community, completely dependent for its livelihood on the potato crop which was harvested annually. At one point in time, potato production in Maine outstripped that of Idaho by 20%. When I was a teenager there, most of the crop was still harvested by hand (and backs and legs!) by the local population. The school year revolved around the harvest: we started our yearly studies in mid-August in order for the schools to close in mid-September so that the children could help bring in the crop. (It was only later, when I was in university studying sociology, that I learned of the 'deprived' area of northern Maine which still used 'child labour' in order to bring in the autumn harvest.)

It was not just the schools that adjusted their operations to the crop, but other community activities were oriented alongside the phases of seeding, crop development and harvesting. Each June saw the annual 'Potato Blossom Festival', with the crowning of the Potato Blossom Festival Queen; there was a fair trade in recipe books with potatoes as their main ingredient, and shops sold clothing and equipment that would be necessary for all stages of the crop's development.

My memory of that time in my life – along with that of a sore back and hard work – was of being part of a community working outdoors together. This sense culminated each year with the bringing in of the harvest, an endeavour in which the entire community was engaged. As dawn broke over September mornings, farmers collected their 'pickers' in dilapidated old school buses or trucks, transporting them to fields already alive with the sound of the 'digger', the contraption hauled by a tractor over adjacent rows of potatoes which dug the tubers and shook them along racks of metal trays before depositing them onto the top of dark brown earth.

Farmers allocated each of us a 'section' of field which was the responsibility of each child or young adult to 'pick', and the aim was to have picked up all of your section of potatoes (in baskets that were then dumped into 250-pound barrels which you tagged with your picker number) before the digger returned to unearth and drop another two rows of potatoes. Older teenage boys drove trucks which circulated throughout the fields, hoisting the barrels onto the flat beds, and then driving off to deposit the crop into barns or delivering them direct to market. It was noisy, back-breaking and potentially dangerous work (each harvest was inevitably accompanied by broken limbs and sometimes even deaths in the meeting of man with machines.) But it was also the arena for potato field romances, communal lunches of bologna and mustard on soft white bread, potato field battles, and the sense of shared exhilaration and relief when a twenty-acre field was successfully harvested.

Memories of that time are rife with the feeling of being part of a larger, cyclical rhythm as well as the dawning realisation of the interdependency between us as a human community and the Earth itself. Although the work was hard, it physically connected us to the land and to one another. To this day, on autumn mornings when I get the whiff of overturned earth, I am immediately transported back to northern Maine and those early mornings waiting for potatoes to reveal themselves from the ground. The memory is always accompanied by a feeling of comfort and connection, and a sense of perspective in really feeling my place among the other creatures and forces of the world.

The second key aspect of growing up in Caribou was the extent to which my brother and sister lived out of doors. Apart from our time in school, we were outside. During the summer we ran in the fields that backed on to our house, learning where the patches of wild strawberries grew thick and chasing prairie dogs back into their holes. We took excursions to the nearby lakes and spent whole days dipping in and out of the icy waters and exploring the woods that surrounded them. Winters were long and cold, but we took advantage of the snow and ice by skiing downhill on nearby slopes, or skating at the town's ice rink. We were wild children, as were our friends, growing up knowing the habits of the plants and the animals, the length of time it took to cycle to any part of town, the most opportune spaces to rest where the blackflies wouldn't congregate. We knew the different kinds of 'cold', the kind that meant you needed to wear a balaclava as well as a hat, or that which you could survive wearing only woollen mittens rather than a double layer of gloves.

I am not trying to paint a picture of an idyllic childhood. There were disturbances, prejudices, rivalries and feuds as there are in any close-knit provincial community. But there was also a sense of physical spaciousness, balanced by our growing knowledge of a defined place and the sense of learning how to fend for ourselves as creatures of that place. When I recall my time in Caribou, those memories are alive with a fulsome awareness of what it is to inhabit a place. We walked or rode our bikes everywhere. I knew that place, and somehow, the place seemed to know me, too. Trees had boughs at just the right height in which I could perch to read my beloved books, materials were available for the hut my brother built himself in the field, a cabin where he slept overnight and concocted plots with his other boy mates. The snow formed itself, with our help, into ice caves suitable for sitting in.

It is this very personal experience of inhabiting a particular place as a child which informs my subsequent more intellectual constructions of 'humans' and 'the natural world' and how we might experience well-being through that relationship. Whenever my ideas become too lofty, I return to memories of the many hours I sat in the branch of the tree I thought of as 'mine', and the simple feeling of pleasure it gave me then still wafts through my bones. However, there are authors whose works have provided me with new ways of thinking about this vital connection, and why it might be so. I offer some of their ideas here in the hope that they might enrich this territory and bring additional insight to what happens in the meeting of human and more-than-human worlds.

I begin that exploration with the French phenomenologist[1] Maurice Merleau-Ponty. In particular, I suggest that through this philosopher's understanding of the nature of human embodiment, a novel relationship between the more-than-human world and human beings can be constructed. I believe his radical philosophy can serve as the ground for an appreciation of the nature of human well-being and the role the 'natural environment' plays in its realisation.

Maurice Merleau-Ponty and the natural environment

The French phenomenologist Maurice Merleau-Ponty is recognised as having expanded the field of possibility for thinking about the embodied aspect of being human more than any other philosopher. The starting point for Merleau-Ponty's project is to critique and reappraise Descartes' conceptualisation of the human 'being' as split between mind and body aspects. In his search for the ultimate ground of certainty, Descartes' 'cogito ergo sum' (colloquially known as 'I think therefore I am', but possibly more accurately rendered as 'I know myself to be a thinking being') located certitude as something which can only be determined by the rational aspects of human knowing. Consequent to this formulation, rationality – or in Cartesian terms, the transcendent aspects of being human – took precedence over more embodied, sensually-based ways of knowing.

Merleau-Ponty disagrees with Descartes' analysis, and instead posits an ontology[2] of human being in which the material, 'immanent' aspect of human corporeality and the transcendent,[3] rational, imaginal aspects of humanness are inherently and inescapably intertwined. Merleau-Ponty argues that consciousness is not, and cannot be 'disembodied'. Our very means of perception depends on the physical aspects of the materiality of our eyes, as well as on the way in which we are geographically and spatially located in the world.

Much of Merleau-Ponty's argument is based on his exacting study of perception, both from a philosophic and an empirical point of view. The key aspects of his philosophy of perception are presented in his book *The Phenomenology of Perception* published in 1945, but another text, *The Visible and the Invisible*, published after the philosopher's death in 1961, developed these core ideas further. A central notion to his concept of perception is that of 'reversibility'. Merleau-Ponty notes that key to human being in the world is the fact that we are 'percipient perceptibles'. That is, just as we can see, we are seen. Our being in the world is essentially one of reversibility, seeing and of being seen.

This is a relatively straightforward concept when considering humans perceiving and being perceived by other humans. But Merleau-Ponty stretches the bounds of how we might understand reversibility by suggesting that as 'phenomenal things' in a world of other 'phenomenal things', it is not just other human eyes that 'perceive' us.

Dillon explains this by writing:

> (There is) . . . a fundamental reflexivity in the lived body's relations with worldly objects, such that every contact with a thing is at the same time a presence to itself; I cannot touch an object without being touched by it, and indeed, eye-hand co-ordination without this kind of corporeal reflexivity would be impossible'. (p.143)

In other words, according to Merleau-Ponty, reversibility occurs not just between ourselves and other humans, but between us and the 'more-than-human' world as well. Merleau-Ponty illustrates this experience by writing in his essay 'Eye and Mind' (1964) about a painter who describes his experience of painting in a forest:

> In a forest I have felt many times over that it was not I who was looking at the forest. I felt on certain days that it was rather the trees that were looking at me. (p.167)

I would suggest that Merleau-Ponty is not here arguing that trees have

'eyes' and can literally 'see' the painter. Instead, he is drawing to our attention the interrelationship between seeing and being seen. The painter in
the wood knows himself, not only through his agentic[4] ability to perceive
the trees and paint them, but through how he knows himself to 'be' in
relation to the trees. He is not as tall as the trees, for instance, nor is his
girth as wide. Although both he and the trees share an upward orientation
in respect to the earth, the extension of the trees' branches is broader, the
sound the wind makes as it rustles through the trees' leaves is different
from that produced by the wind nudging the painter's body.

Merleau-Ponty's ontology of perception suggests a strong inter-connec-
tion between humans and how humans come to know themselves and the
more-than-human world. In very real ways, humans depend on the phenomenal world for their sense of self-knowledge and identity. The more-
than-human world is the always present 'other' through which I know
myself, my capabilities as well as my limitations. It teaches me where I fit
into the larger community of beings. This relationship is highlighted by the
quote which opens this chapter, written by a Native American of the Creek
Nation, Joy Harjo.

To return to the story of my time in Caribou, Maine, in a similar way
part of the significance of being a member of an agricultural community was
that I got to know myself through the cycle of growing and harvesting food.
In coming to know the natural rhythms of planting time, blossom time, and
harvest, I learned analogously about my own rhythms and requirements for
rest, nourishment and production. Through the community's activities associated with producing its livelihood, I came to know myself both in terms of
how 'I fit' within the social community, but I also came to learn more about
myself vis-à-vis the larger, more-than-human community. Just as my parents
and teachers and the farmer I worked for informed of me 'who I was' and
'how I fitted into my family, my school, and my work', the fields in which I
worked told me about my physical capacity to work, the sky I woke up to
told me of my capacity for delight in the colours of its changing topography,
the weather told me of my limits for cold and wetness, the number of barrels of spuds I could pick told me about my strength and also grew me as I
transported potatoes from ground to barrel.

An important aspect of my engagement with Caribou, and with the
potato harvest there, was that as well as knowing in my body the way in
which I as an individual, and we as a community, relied on the more-than-
human world for our food and livelihood, I was also aware of the impact

I and we had on the earth itself. I was aware at a visceral level of the 'inter-penetration' of the world and me. To develop further the nature of that interconnection I turn to the idea of 'dwelling', as constructed by the phenomenologist Martin Heidegger.

Heidegger's notion of dwelling

In saving the earth, in receiving the sky, in awaiting the divinities, in initiating the mortals, dwelling occurs as the fourfold preservation of the fourfold.
– Heidegger, 'Building Dwelling Thinking', p.151

Heidegger wrote his essay 'Building Dwelling Thinking' at the end of the second world war, when Germany was in the midst of a significant housing crisis. Elsewhere, he wrote of the pain experienced by "German women picking through the rubble of demolished German cities". So there was a very practical, lived situation which underpinned his quest to understand the nature of 'dwelling' from a philosophical perspective.

In constructing his argument, Heidegger posits that to be human, is, at its most essential, to dwell. But dwelling, which in German is the word '*bauen*', has a much deeper meaning than that we colloquially associate with it. He explains:

> The old word *bauen* to which (the word) *bin* belongs, answers: *ich bin, du bist* meaning: I dwell, you dwell. The way in which you are and I am, the manner in which humans are on the earth, is '*bauen*', or dwelling. To be a human being means to be on the earth as a mortal. It means to dwell. . . . this word *bauen* also means to cherish and protect, to preserve and care for, specifically to till the soil, to cultivate the vine... (1971, p.147)

Essential to Heidegger's notion of dwelling is the idea of participation. Dwelling denotes a relationship of interdependency in which both the place in which dwelling occurs, and the 'dweller' herself, are altered by their interaction. To return to my own example of home, the snowhuts which my siblings and I inhabited were altered and built through our work and agency: we dug into snowdrifts and hollowed out space with our hands. However, the snow made its impact on us as well: our fingers froze, our backs curved with the effort of shifting snow. In this way, dwelling is participative, rather than being a one-way process.

A further important feature of Heidegger's construction is that he proposes that dwelling means to "cherish and protect, preserve and care for". In fact the notion of preserving and caring for is core to Heidegger's notion, but the caring for has a different connotation from that often connected to constructions of caring. It is not so much a caring which asks the carer to 'sort out' a problem or fix some aspect of what is being cared for. Instead, the quality of caring Heidegger sees as essential to dwelling is one which enables the other to reveal itself. Dwelling enables the opening of a space in which the other can come into its own presence with the carer. This is quite a difficult notion, but one which I believe is worth pursuing a bit further.

As mentioned earlier, for Heidegger notions of dwelling centre around the possibility of 'caring for'. Again, in 'Building Dwelling Thinking' he writes:

> Mortals dwell in that they save the earth – but here saving means 'to set something free into its own presencing'.* To save the earth is more than to exploit it or even wear it out. Saving the earth does not master the earth and does not subjugate it, which is merely one step from spoliation. (p.150)

This quote seems particularly apt in today's context, in which we are exhorted to 'save the planet' through reduced energy usage and recycling efforts. How might we approach this endeavour in a way aligned with Heidegger's idea of saving?

One way of fostering such a capability might be through engaging with the notion of 'comportment'. In his essay 'The Essence of Truth' (2002) Heidegger described comportment as a way of 'standing open to beings', an open way of holding oneself in relation to the other. He elaborates on this, writing:

> Every open relatedness is a comportment. Man's open stance varies depending on the kind of beings and the way of comportment. All working and achieving, all action and calculation, keep within an open region within which beings, with regard to what they are and how they are can properly take their stand and become capable of being said. (p.122)

The way one comports oneself is essential for creating a space in which entities, either human, or more-than-human, can reveal themselves as they truly are. This 'sparing' things we encounter to be free is central to Heidegger's notion of 'care'. This way of being is perhaps illustrated by reference to another story, this time one told by the American environmental

---

* For Heidegger, presencing means to 'make present' or a disclosing of the essence of, in this case, the earth.

philosophers Cheney and Weston (1999). They describe a situation in which a camera crew is brought into an animal testing lab to record a television programme. The researcher who is there to take notes as the filming occurs quickly becomes interested by the different approaches taken by the film actors, scientists working with the animals, and the animals' carers, vis-à-vis the animals.

She notes that the film crew barely relate to the animals at all: they don't seem to notice them as distinct creatures with individual ways of being. The scientists interact with the animals in a distanced, prescribed way, and although they take more care with the animals than do the actors, their interest seems boundaried by their own purposes and concerns. The animal carers, however, are distinctive in the way they interact with the animals. They seem to see each creature as an individual, and relate to it in a specific and nuanced way. The carers provoke different responses from the animals than do the actors or the scientists: the researcher notes how the animals visibly relax under their care and become more energised and lively.

Cheney and Weston suggest the carers interact with the animals in a way which embodies respect, and go on to argue that such an orientation is one which is in keeping with an environmental ethic of etiquette. This way of being, or 'comportment', to use Heidegger's term, recognises the essential 'personhood' of the other, be they human or more-than-human. Such respect, I propose, is one of the foundations for relationships between humans and the more-than-human world which would foster well-being on both sides. For again, if Merleau-Ponty's notion of reversibility has any validity, it would suggest that in fostering interactions in which the other is more present, one can come to know oneself more fulsomely also. Paradoxically, dwelling would suggest that such self-knowing is not necessarily accomplished through steadfast self-expression and application of one's agency, but through creating an open space, in which the other can reveal him, her, or itself.

In drawing this section of the chapter to a close, I'd like to return to Heidegger's concern with dwelling. In the final paragraphs of his essay 'Building Dwelling Thinking', Heidegger poses the question: 'What is the state of dwelling in our precarious age?' His answer seems to resonate with our own times, some seventy years later:

> However hard and bitter, however hampering and threatening the lack of houses remains, the real plight of dwelling does not lie merely with the lack of houses.

The real plight of dwelling is indeed older than the world wars with their destruction, older than the increase of the earth's population and the condition of the industrial workers. The real dwelling plight lies in this, that mortals ever search anew for the nature of dwelling, that they must ever learn to dwell. What if man's homelessness consisted in this, that man still does not even think of the real plight of dwelling as the plight? Yet as soon as man gives thought to his homelessness, it is a misery no longer. Rightly considered and kept well in mind, it is the sole summons that calls mortals into their dwelling. (p.161)

This quote seems especially apt for our particular times, as we face a growing environmental crisis which threatens not just our ability to live in houses, but to live on the very Earth itself. How might 'dwelling' enable us to respond well to the ecological crisis of our times, in a way which contributes to both human well-being and that of the planet? According to Heidegger, dwelling is essentially about caring and preserving. It is about understanding 'our place' amidst what Heidegger calls "the fourfold", the earth, the sky, the divinities and the mortals. But what might that mean in applied terms? To explore this, I turn to the very practical work being undertaken in communities across the world to restore broken and misused landscapes.

Restoration and re-habitation: co-created means of achieving well-being for both humans and the more-than-human world

As mentioned previously, central to Heidegger's notion of dwelling is the idea of participation. In order to develop human well-being, we cannot just think our way through to ethical relations with the more-than-human world, we must engage in action. But here I am suggesting that the nature of that action is critical. If that action is based in an agentic sense of mastery and knowing 'what is best', I would suggest that it will fall foul of fostering truly participative engagement conducive to well-being in humans or the more-than-human world. How might we conceive of such action, which is directed towards certain purposes, but also remains responsive to the particular qualities, needs and projects of 'the other'?

This is the dilemma at the heart of much environmental philosophy writing concerning the human activity of restoring damaged landscapes. Although one would expect that restoration attempts would be applauded by environmental philosophers, there is in fact a good deal of debate about the ethics of restoration practices. Part of the dissent is based on the idea that restoration often is done with human purposes in mind, and disregards the land's 'own projects' and potential possibilities (Katz 1992). Furthermore, restoration can be seen as an attempt to 'fake' more 'natural' processes, and in fact it is argued that the intrinsic value of landscape which has never been altered by human intervention, either through despoiling it or through restoring it, will always be greater than that of tampered-with land (Elliot 1982).

There is a different view, however, which is inherent in the work of more activist-oriented environmentalists such as Stephanie Mills, whose book *In Service of the Wild* speaks eloquently to the potential healing aspects of human involvement with the land in efforts to restore it. In her book, she recounts case studies of successful 'reinhabitation' projects, including the restoration of Illinois' savannah and prairie lands, the reintroduction and support of wild salmon in the Pacific Northwest, and 'greenwork' being undertaken in Auroville, a 25-year-old intentional community in India, in which countless hours of volunteer work have been used to restore despoiled areas or species.

Mills is careful to distinguish between ideas of 'restoration', which can often involve restoring a landscape to some historical idyll or human centred project, and 'reinhabitation', which involves coming to know a particular landscape for 'itself'. Her idea of reinhabitation seems to resonate with Heidegger's view of 'caring and preserving', for it involves engaging with broken landscapes in a way which is sensitive to the original intents of the land itself.

The possibility of developing this kind of sensitivity is illustrated in a story Mills tells about Steve Packard, the Director of a savannah and prairie regeneration project in northern Illinois. Starting from the belief that an area surrounded by oak forest 'should have been' prairie, Packard began a planting project to regenerate typical prairie plants. But they didn't take. Instead, what Packard referred to as 'a few oddball species' which were neither forest nor prairie began to grow. By engaging in 'some masterful sleuthing', as Mills calls it, Packard was able to piece together a different view of the 'original' intent of the land. He started to speculate about the kinds of plant which would have flourished in the midst of the oak canopy. Through historic and taxonomic databases, he was able to identify the 'oddball species' and create a list of plants more typical of savannah than prairie landscape. When these plants were introduced to the area, they thrived and produced a flourishing savannah ecology. But this only occurred through Packard's willingness to attend to and respond to 'what the land was trying to tell him'.

Mills elaborates on the difference between restoration and reinhabitation in this way:

> Restoration implies an exacting fidelity to the original; reinhabitation may resort to the use of similar species in order to create a rough, but functional semblance of the original ecosystem. Restoration presently, and in many cases necessarily, requires that access to the recovering ecosystem be restricted, rather like a burn-ward of a hospital. Reinhabitation implies living in, and having an economic stake in, the place restored, not in the touristic sense of being able to charge admission at the park gate, but in being able to derive what House calls 'natural provision' from one's own ground: free (but not easy) protein, fuel, and building material. Restoration does not pose an alternative to the socio-economic system which is necessitating restoration, reinhabitation does. (1995, p. 160).

Perhaps this quote serves to bring the chapter full circle, in that it alludes to the benefits which human beings might enjoy from participation in such reinhabitation projects, in the form of 'natural provision'. I would suggest that reinhabitation can bring us into contact with much more than the physical ground of our well-being, although knowing where our sustenance comes from is certainly a fundamental part of that well-being. But, as the story of my own connection with home I hope highlighted, that kind of engagement can be an essential way in which one's sense of identity as part of a larger, planetary community as well as a social one is formed. In this way, reinhabitation – dwelling, if you will – provides the means for coming to know our place among the more-than-human world, and through a direct experience of that interconnection, can foster a (literally!) grounded sense of well-being.

Concluding thoughts

In this chapter I have presented a way of thinking of human well-being as intimately linked to engagement with and appreciation of our connection with the more-than-human world. In forming this argument, I've drawn from the philosophical ideas of two twentieth-century philosophers, Merleau-Ponty and Heidegger, focusing particularly on their ideas of reversibility and dwelling, respectively. The notion of dwelling has been further elaborated by considering the practice of re-inhabitation, a way of engaging with the more-than-human world in a way which seeks to respond sensitively to its own 'projects'. But what might all of this mean for each of us, as many of us live in urban and suburban communities cut off from agricultural practices or even the possibility of having a nearby savannah to restore?

Today I live in the suburban community of Milton Keynes, an hour's drive north of London. It is a far cry from my childhood home in Caribou, Maine. It is a 'new town', built primarily to accommodate people who work in London, and it is known in the UK for its extensive road system dotted by frequent 'roundabouts', or 'traffic circles'. How might I, living in this almost totally man-made environment connect and engage with the 'more-than-human' world in a way that could foster the well-being of us both?

My answer to this has both a philosophical and a practical response. Philosophically, I return to the argument with which the chapter opened, about the extent to which humans and the natural world should be seen as distinct entities. Although Milton Keynes is largely 'man-made', in that it is a planned conurbation, the thousands of trees which line its streets grow, give shade, and provide homes to communities of bugs and birds, as do their counterparts in more 'natural' landscapes. The city's planners have been kind in retaining large tracts of undeveloped land, open spaces where humans can play and relax in the sun, as well as providing allotment areas where we suburban dwellers can grow our own vegetables and flowers. Although not all man-made environments have been as carefully constructed to encourage interaction between the human and more-than-human worlds, I would suggest that if we stop conceptualising them as separate entities, we can be more alert to their overlap even in the most urban of landscapes. In other words, the more-than-human world is our constant companion, no matter where we live, and it is always available for us to relate to and communicate with if we are but attentive to its presence.

Practically, the way 'dwelling' infuses my life in a more actively conscious way is through the simple, everyday practice of walking out of doors. My husband and I will soon be joined by a puppy to accompany us on these daily outings, an addition to our household which is in part rooted in our desire to spend some time outdoors every day, whatever the weather. The dog who previously shared our lives probably taught me more about dwelling than I could ever learn from Heidegger or Merleau-Ponty. His constant delight at the smells, sounds and tastes of whatever the world offered him taught me how to be attentive to the small and subtle ways in which the world constantly expresses itself. During our years of morning and evening walks, I found myself grow increasingly more attuned to the daily changes in flora, slight alterations in temperature and wind, smells which alerted me to the presence of new blossom or other creatures – all simple and often unconscious 'knowings' which fed my sense of connectedness with the more-than-human world. For me anyway, this sense of connectedness provides the ground for my sense of well-being, not only because it helps me to feel not so alone, but also through the widened perspective it offers, constantly reminding me of my place within the greater family of all things.

* * *

References

D. Abram (1996) *The Spell of the Sensuous: Perception and Language in a More-than-Human World*, Pantheon, New York.

J. Cheney and A. Weston (1999) 'Environmental ethics as environmental etiquette: Towards an ethics-based epistemology', *Environmental Ethics* 21, pp.120-136.

M.C. Dillon (1997) *Merleau-Ponty's Ontology* (2nd Edition), Northwestern University Press, Evanston, Illinois.

R. Elliot (1982) 'Faking Nature', *Inquiry* 25, pp.81-93.

M. Heidegger (1971) *Poetry, Language, Thought* (A. Hofstadter, trans.), Harper Colophon Books, New York, pp.145-161.

M. Heidegger (2002) 'On the Essence of Truth' in *Basic Writings*, David Farrell Krell (ed.) 6th edition, Routledge, London, pp.111-138.

E. Katz (1992) 'The Big Lie: Human Restoration of Nature', *Research in Philosophy and Technology* 12, pp.93-107.

M. Merleau-Ponty (1962) *Phenomenology of Perception* (C. Smith, trans.), Routledge, London.

M. Merleau-Ponty (1964) 'Eye and Mind' (C. Dallery, trans.) in *The Primacy of Perception*, J. M. Edie (ed.), Northwestern University Press, Evanston, Illinois.

M. Merleau-Ponty (1968) *The Visible and the Invisible*, Northwestern University Press, Evanston, Illinois.

S. Mills (1995) *In Service of the Wild: Restoring and Reinhabiting Damaged Land*, Beacon Press, Boston.

Notes

1. Taken literally, phenomenology is simply the study (or philosophy) of 'phenomena' such as the appearances of things, or things as they appear in our experience including the ways we experience them. Phenomenology also refers to the meanings things have in our experience.

2. Ontology refers to the philosophical study of existence, of what 'is'.

3. What is embodied and what transcends, goes beyond, human existence as manifested bodily.

4. Agentic – exercising the capacity to act in the world.

Chapter Seven

Emmaus: homes for the homeless

by Lucy Thompson

'Together in diversity' – Abbé Pierre

Emmaus is based on the principle of the meeting of two worlds, and of these two worlds converging towards a goal of the common good. Abbé Pierre, the founder of Emmaus, said that at its fundamental soul it was a meeting of "a few people that we might consider to be among the privileged and more fortunate members of society with a few people from the ranks of the less fortunate, united in looking towards other distresses and deciding to combine forces."[1]

Built around the founding principles of universal solidarity and equity, Emmaus' central activity is to fight exclusion. Founded in post-war France in response to the plight of homeless individuals, it has expanded to become an international movement. Its not inconsiderable aim is to "help through our action, every man, every society and every nation to live, assert and fulfil itself through communication and sharing and with equal dignity".[2] To furnish an understanding of Emmaus, this chapter will look at its history, the problems Emmaus was responding to, and the philosophy that grew from this. It will then look at a couple of examples of communities, from the developed and from the developing world and the links between these.

The birth of Emmaus

Emmaus is a secular organisation consisting of self-sustaining communities providing a place to live and work for previously homeless people. They are autonomous communities bounded by a set of principles which assert that every person is of value, is equal, and that as "a united community anyone will only be judged by their human qualities, *here and now*".[3] The communities finance themselves by the collecting, recycling and selling on of goods. An individual on arrival at a community will have to work a 40-hour week in one aspect of the community's work, sign off any benefits that they are receiving, and abide by the rule of no drink or drugs on the premises. What the individual is offered in return is a non-judgemental atmosphere in which to regain confidence, self-esteem and a sense of freedom. There is no limit on the amount of time that a person can stay at Emmaus – from a week to a lifetime – this giving the security to grow in confidence. Originating in France, Emmaus now has 317 member associations based in 36 countries in Africa, America, Asia and Europe. The communities are involved in hugely diverse activities, which I will touch on later, but the central principles remain the same.

To understand the principles by which the community lives it will be helpful to look at the history of Emmaus and at the man who founded the movement, Abbé Pierre, whose philosophy permeates the organisation.

Abbé Pierre, born Henry Groues in Lyon in 1912, was a charismatic French priest, frequently voted France's most popular Frenchman until his death in 2007. He has been likened as a mixture of Asterix and David, of Goliath fame,[4] for his willingness to take on authority to fight injustice and inequality. An active member of the Resistance during the second world war, he became a symbol of the fight against Nazi oppression. Though ordained into the Catholic Church in 1938, he courted controversy by openly voicing dissent on elements of its teaching and practice – including its hierarchical nature, its ban on contraception and on the ordination of women. Abbé Pierre was a rebel against a system he perceived to be resting on its laurels, and a man who believed that things could be different. Feeling keenly the injustices and inequalities of society, he believed that it was his place, and the place of Emmaus, to act as "a provocation to the general conscience of society".[5]

After the war Abbé Pierre became a member of parliament, and in 1947 he rented a house in Neuilly Plaisance on the outskirts of Paris. It was a large house, larger than he needed, and seeing the disillusionment of the young following the nihilism and destruction of war he opened up a youth hostel in his house aimed at creating international reconciliation and solidarity. He named it Emmaus, after the biblical story in which the disciples regained hope after the death of Jesus. At this time the Abbé was also engaged in building homes for the homeless, due to a housing shortage following the war. The pivotal moment in the emergence of Emmaus, though, was in 1949 when the Abbé was called to a see a man who had just tried to commit suicide. In response to the man's despair he asked if he would help him in building the homes for the homeless. The man, Georges, agreed and came to live at Emmaus to help with the Abbé's building programme. Georges became the first 'companion', as people living and working at Emmaus came to be known. By asking the man to help there became a reason for his existence, and it is this attitude that is the essence of Emmaus – the empowering request for help that assumes a confidence and respect for the person. In the words of the Emmaus UK slogan, it is giving "homeless people a bed and a reason to get out of it".

Many dispossessed people subsequently turned up at the Abbé's home looking for shelter, companionship and work. The community was financed by the Abbé's parliamentary salary until 1951, the year in which he resigned. Falling on hard times, the Abbé, unbeknownst to the others, started begging on the streets of Paris for money. On hearing this, the companions felt it compromised their and the Abbé's self-respect, and it was one of the companions that suggested another way of earning money, through ragpicking. Ragpicking meant the collecting of people's unwanted goods and sifting rubbish tips for reclaimable items, then repairing the goods and selling them on. This occupation financed the community, with self-sufficiency becoming a central tenet to the organisation.

During a particularly cold winter in 1954 the community rose to greater prominence. The combination of the cold and lack of housing was resulting in needless deaths. The community responded by providing temporary shelter for people, and the Abbé made an emotive appeal on the radio for support from the French people. The resulting response was known as the 'goodwill uprising', which had the effect of mobilising the government to support house building that had been refused earlier, supplying 10 billion francs of funds to build 12,000 emergency homes immediately throughout France for the most underprivileged.

These events were the origins of the international movement of today, but at its root and that which informs the whole movement was the meeting in 1949 of the privileged man and the less fortunate man. Abbé Pierre was keen to emphasise the human element as the core constituent of Emmaus, which has continued to evolve organically from the simple belief of reaching out, that the liberation of the self comes through helping others.

'A contagion of deeds'

The open and non-judgemental philosophy of Abbé Pierre has been a driving force of the Emmaus movement. Starting as a reaction to the plight of the French homeless, Emmaus has grown to encompass a "struggle against exclusion"[6] in all its manifestations. Abbé Pierre believed that the one practical action of reaching out to another person had the potential to enable a fairer world through a 'contagion of deeds'.[7] His refreshing and liberating disregard for the status quo encompassed a belief that society and the systems of advantage and disadvantage can be changed for the better through action. This was not true of any one country, but was a global vision. In an editorial from 1973, the Abbé said that we should refer to the "whole world as our countries",[8] meaning by this that no country's peoples are of less value and that existing international inequalities are unacceptable. In this editorial he mentions that if the international inequities that exist are not enough to move people's conscience, which in his view they should be, should they not be moved by these facts in order to safeguard smooth future international relations? This is a pertinent point for times in which increased demands on resources and climate change will potentially cause conflict.

The spirit of inclusion as embodied in Emmaus attracted the attention of people throughout the world who were trying to fight similar issues, and resulted in various communities being set up. Abbé Pierre travelled to many of the regions involved to help with advice. In 1971 Emmaus International was formally set up with 70 different groups in 20 countries. The organisation has a decentralised structure based round the promotion of international solidarity, while each community is individually autonomous; the communities themselves originate in the decision of local people to form a group.

Emmaus groups can be residential communities, working communities, or social welfare structures, and the activities that each community is involved in vary widely due to the different local contexts. Communities in Europe centre around the reprocessing of goods and sheltering of community members. They are engaged in various social projects: for example housing, helping people with disabilities and promoting fair trade. African Emmaus groups focus on the needs of young people, women and rural populations, and are more likely to be engaged in farming, market gardening and livestock rearing. American groups tend to be based around the reprocessing of goods and projects that they are involved in centre round education, training, hygiene and healthcare. Asia has a huge range of projects, from helping the homeless and people with disabilities in South Korea, to training of women and *dalits* in India, through to providing people in the Lebanon with micro-credit. There are also mutual health and education funds in Africa and America, a system by which members of an Emmaus group can make a monthly payment in order to have affordable access to these services. It is important to emphasise that there is a vast range of projects, and that these cannot be neatly pigeonholed by region. It is action to empower those who are socially excluded to regain control of their lives and to help those that suffer for whatever reason.

The foundation of the international movement is the communities themselves, but they work and raise money for specific projects agreed by the world assembly, which is formed of representatives from each region. Abbé Pierre compared the organisation to a tree, and at its 'roots' are the communities of ragpickers. Agreed projects will be supported by all communities through solidarity actions and finance. The community and international solidarity is best illustrated using examples of these communities and the issues that they face: showing how the excluded homeless man in a city in the UK can benefit, as can the mother living in poverty in Benin in west Africa.

The ragpickers of the UK

There are currently 14 communities in the UK, and several more in the pipeline. The first community was set up in 1992 in Cambridge, and there are now thriving communities from Glasgow to Brighton. All UK communities are residential and based round the recycling of unwanted goods and selling these on in the Emmaus shop, with a few of them also running cafés for visitors. The central problem Emmaus is dealing with in the UK is homelessness. Much work in the more affluent countries focuses on helping and supporting previously homeless people. The combination of a materially wasteful society with a dislocated homeless population means that the collecting and recycling of goods has greater potential to make a difference in these countries as compared with the more impoverished areas of the world.

Homelessness affects around 380,000 people in the UK. The reasons for people finding themselves homeless are various, and according to the charity Crisis include:[9]

- Time in local authority care
- Contact with criminal justice system
- Previous service in the Armed Forces
- Alcohol and drug misuse
- Mental health problems
- Experience of abuse
- Disputes with parents or step-parents
- Marital or relationship breakdown
- Domestic violence
- Bereavement
- Lack of social support networks
- Learning difficulties
- Exclusion from school
- Unemployment

Fundamentally, homelessness is caused by a breakdown of relationships and a lack of community, meaning that in the event of a crisis a person has no one to fall back on. The problem is that people finding themselves in this situation will find it difficult to get out of it. The exclusion from society, the casual dismissiveness of strangers, the lack of hope can mean a downward spiral, and in many cases can lead to substance abuse as a means of escape. Crucially, then, the problems of homelessness are so much more than about housing. In the report 'Homelessness and Loneliness', Gerard Lemos talks of the problems of homelessness as a "want of conviviality"[10] brought on by a lack of access to, or breakdown in, relationships with a core family network or a more extended network. To bring a person out of this situation in any permanent sense requires that this 'conviviality' be there, or the person will lapse into his or her previous life. Exclusion is a social rather than economic construct.

As a result of their situation, the homeless may embrace a 'negative freedom'[11] as a reaction to their lack of self-determination. The person who starts with the universal desire for happiness and the means by which to attain this, realises a lack of control over their life, and in reaction to this chooses to avoid defeat and disappointment, striving for nothing that they cannot be sure to attain. As a result a person will be in a vicious circle of low expectation and low self-esteem.

What by contrast, Emmaus can offer, through physical succour and conviviality, is 'positive freedom' so that the person may feel that their life once again is self-determined, not at the mercy of external forces, becoming conscious of themselves as 'a thinking, willing, active being, bearing responsibility for my choices and able to explain them by reference to my own ideas and purposes'.[12] It is from this position of strength that Emmaus gives people a new life. It is the network of human relationships that provides the real strength, which was why Abbé Pierre emphasised the small human contacts. Centrally, Emmaus is about giving trust and respect to an individual who has lost a sense of self-respect; this is immensely empowering, since people so often live up to the expectations of themselves and can be as Fritz Schumacher, the author of *Small is Beautiful*, noted, "destroyed by the inner conviction of uselessness".[13]

The Emmaus community offers support through community and work. In the UK, an individual working in a community can expect to work in one aspect of community life, which could mean refurbishing items in the workshop, sorting donated items, working in the customer café or serving customers in the shop. The pay is between £30 and £37 a week, with £6 put into savings for if/when they leave, and it is a 40-hour week. Communities encourage people to take holidays, and provide allowance for this and travel expenses. This way of life is obviously not the answer for all people who find themselves homeless, but should they be willing to commit to this, it offers the security, support, companionship and training to empower them to make the necessary transformative changes within their lives. One previous companion said that it is not a sanctuary from real life, but that it could be said to be taking it on head-on.[14] The emphasis is on the power of meaningful work, friendship, social activities and practical assistance. This is not as a means to an end, though, but rather can be an end in itself if people wish to stay. There is no requirement for people to move on. The security of Emmaus is that a person can stay for as long or as a short a time as they wish, and in the UK the average person stays just over six months, but 33% stay for two years or over.

Benefits to the wider society

Emmaus UK states that any community must not be set up in isolation but must be seen as part of the wider community to which it will add value. It should be a symbiotic relationship, and there are numerous benefits of this relationship. Firstly Emmaus provides a real service, by collecting people's unwanted goods and also offering cheaper goods (in the UK, people on benefits also get a discount). This is not basket weaving for prisoners, but a real working community and provider. It also provides a real environmental service in a throwaway culture. Emmaus will sell anything: from books to bikes, from sofas to saxophones. The companions will fix and clean what they receive; the objects received are often in a good condition but no longer required. In an increasingly wasteful culture, this mass of 'stuff' is a considerable bounty. By reusing these items Emmaus is able to substantially reduce the amount of material that goes to landfill – it is estimated that Emmaus Cambridge reduces this by 925 tonnes per year.[15] The emphasis that Emmaus puts on helping others also means that the communities will actively be involved in local charities. For example, Emmaus Cambridge runs winter soup runs and an initiative in partnership with a local night shelter to redistribute surplus food.

Further than this though, the person shopping or giving goods to Emmaus may find their attitudes challenged and be encouraged to reduce their own consumption and need to buy new. Its shops and cafés also offer a hub of equality and inclusion, and it is not just the companions who will benefit from this but the visitors too. Stereotypes of the homeless may well be defied through interaction and understanding. Elements of feelings of exclusion are not foreign to many people's experience, and through common understanding a more broadminded approach to society can be encouraged by these communities, which can have the effect of 'jolting comfortable attitudes'.[16]

Emmaus also has the potential to show new ecologically sustainable possibilities to people. It shows an aspirational, but possible, synergistic model of social and environmental justice. An example of a UK community that is currently being built with particular emphasis on sustainable building principles is the Green Roof Project in Hampshire. This exciting project is currently being built to strict environmental standards. As well as solar power and a turf roof it will have a biodiverse garden, including a butterfly and bee walk and a bat hibernacula. This standard will work as an invaluable model for Emmaus and the wider community through the building, but also provides a place where the companions, locals – and bats – can thrive. Perhaps, if a little romanticised, it can become a place that, as the French sociologist Henri Lefebvre wrote of in another context,

> Demonstrate[s] the breadth and magnificence of the possibilities which are opening out for man, and which are so really possible, so near, so rationally achievable (once the political obstacles are shattered) that this proximity of what is possible can only be taken for one of the meanings (painfully and frighteningly unconscious) of the famous 'modern disquiet', the anguish caused by 'existence' as it still is.[17]

So, if this is how Emmaus works for the companions and for the immediate society around it, how does it connect to the wider international community through Emmaus International?

Emmaus International – a global network

As mentioned above, there are Emmaus communities throughout the world dealing with a vast array of different social circumstances. The autonomy of the local groups enables them to deal with the issues from local knowledge – very much from a grassroots standpoint. However, what each Emmaus does supply for the other is the support necessary for each group to flourish. The local groups will see what the needs of the area are, they will raise this with the regions who will research the matters further, and subsequently it will be put to the World Council on Political Action and International Solidarity (made up of representatives from the regions) who meet yearly. They will decide on how the funds are allocated. These funds come from the daily work of the groups, from special sales that each Emmaus community has, and also the Emmaus Salon in Paris. This last is a sale set up by the different community groups that happens every year in Paris specifically for Emmaus International.

There are three main types of solidarity action: these are local action, emergency action and sending containers. Local action involves support of Emmaus initiatives and their partners wherever they are. This could be financing an extension of the Emmaus workshop in Maracanau in Brazil, to a project set up in Lithuania for women who have been trafficked into prostitution to reintegrate them into society. It could mean the buying of computer equipment and training for African Emmaus communities, or a major study into the problems associated with water in India, Bangladesh and Indonesia, which was financed in 2007.

Emmaus have over the last few years provided emergency aid by being involved in reconstruction after the Asian tsunami, providing blankets for Bangladeshis during a particularly cold spell in 2007, and providing micro-credit to people affected in the 2006 war in Lebanon through a partner organisation – the Association d'Entraide Professionnelle (AEP). AEP specialises in micro-credit, supporting small businesses and economic initiatives that people would otherwise be excluded from. Following the war, many of the small businesses were adversely affected, if not entirely incapacitated. Emmaus worked in partnership with the AEP by raising money through the communities, so that people could regain their economic capacity and thereby their self-sufficiency.

The sending of containers is a significant link between more affluent countries and developing countries. As mentioned in the case of the UK, the wealth of the people local to Emmaus communities means that they are well served for goods to sell. Poorer countries do not have this pool of material resources. In view of this, containers of goods are sent from communities with material resources to ones without. In the 2007-8 Emmaus International programme, 60 containers were sent to countries in eastern Europe, Africa, America and Asia. The items sent can then be sold in the receiving community's shop to finance the local group's activities, or used by the local group or partner organisations. It is carefully decided by the receiver and giver in partnership what should be in the container, with members from both communities visiting each other. This is an invaluable resource and an instantly practical realisation of solidarity.

The water companions

One major activity seen as a real priority of Emmaus International is the Nokoué water project. Nokoué is a lake in the west African country of Benin. There are currently five Emmaus groups in Benin. The lake has around 65,000 people living round it or on it in houses on stilts. The area is heavily populated, and drinking water is scarce – there is universal concern about access to water, with 25,000 people having no access to drinkable water at all. Owing to a lack of latrines, there is a problem of the lake becoming an open sewer as human waste is deposited there by people who live along the shoreline in the houses built on stilts. The lake is also being used to dump people's rubbish such as animal carcasses, which has grave implications for water quality, fish stocks and human health. Those people using it to wash or drink are increasingly likely to contract waterborne diseases such as typhoid, dysentery and cholera.

There are few water pumps producing clean water in relation to the population. Isaac Kougbe, a resident of Gbessou, a village on Nokoué, says that life is "permanently searching for water".[18] This task often falls to the women. The women in his village collect water from a point 15 minutes away, the heavy demand meaning that the queue for water can be between three and four hours. This is done twice a day, which obviously has a major impact on the women's lives. According to a United Nations report *Gender Water and Sanitation*, "providing physically accessible clean water is essential for enabling women and girls to devote more time to the pursuit of education, income generation and even the construction and management of water and sanitation facilities."[19] Children are also particularly vulnerable to the adverse effects of water contamination, with long periods out of school due to illness adversely affecting their education and future choices. Choices for the whole community are constrained by this cycle, resulting in the exclusion of people which disempowers them from making positive choices. According to the United Nations, the active education and participation of local people in the management of water is key to the effectiveness of creating sustainable solutions to solving the problems of supply and contamination. In the case of the Emmaus Nokoué water project, this is exactly what is being implemented.

The Nokoué community responded to the situation by contacting the local Emmaus group regarding their water concerns, which has resulted in a scheme to transform the situation by 2010. This will involve 12 new bore wells but also, essentially, education on sanitation to change people's behaviour. As the request came from the local population, so will the project be run as a partnership of the locals, Emmaus and the Sonagnon Association. The project will empower people to make changes in their life, embracing the 'positive freedom' of self-determination. By ownership of the project, its long-term sustainability is far more likely. For the African councillors of Emmaus International, the three main aspects of the project are:

- citizen participation and co-operative management of water
- the right techniques to gain access to drinking water requiring them to be sustainable
- political questioning and advocacy for recognition of water as a fundamental right by Beninese authorities and international decision-makers.

These 'water companions' have been widely supported by Emmaus groups worldwide from other communities in Benin to communities in the UK. In Benin this has included raising awareness amongst women and children about good water management, and selling posters and postcards of Abbé Pierre to raise money for the project. In the UK, Emmaus communities in Bristol, Bolton and Brighton have held exhibitions and talked about Nokoué to local media organisations and schools. They have also organised sales specifically to raise money for the project. Companions have also travelled to Nokoué to help and learn more, and people from Benin have travelled to other communities to raise awareness. It is a bridge of participation linking all the communities. In the view of Patrick Atohoun, a representative of Emmaus International in Africa:

> This project has put on the same road people from the North and people from the South, rich people and poor people. I believe that our world today needs some mixing between different levels of wealth so that at the end of this project we find a man standing up, a man who has access to water.[20]

Emmaus – autonomy and solidarity

This chapter can only hint at the scope of the projects that Emmaus is involved in (for more information on these I can recommend the Emmaus International website and the other national and local websites, details of which are included in the notes at the end of this chapter). What I hope it does get across are the principles of Emmaus, and the exciting vision and reality that it envisages through a combination of empowerment of individuals, solidarity and global equity.

Emmaus works as an invaluable model for sustainability action, encompassing as it does grassroots empowerment with an all-encompassing attitude to the eradication of social exclusion. It has a winning combination of idealism and pragmatism, acting as Abbé Pierre envisaged as a "provocation to the general conscience of society".[21] Its belief in global equity is a belief that is key to fashioning a more sustainable world, embracing difference and sameness and getting away from cycles of blame. The organisation has a very positive attitude, a belief that small actions are important and can make a difference, a faith in the ability to fashion a fairer and more sustainable world.

Emmaus starts from the belief of the absolute value of each individual, but it is the person within the wider society that has meaning. As part of a web of solidarity, the true value of the individual can be realised. From the very roots of Emmaus' beginnings in 1949, when instead of offering charity Abbé Pierre asked for help, the underlying philosophy of Emmaus has been that it is through gaining autonomy that the individual can reach out and gain meaning. Centrally, then, as Le Boursicaud writes, the dispossessed will "not be healed by pity and charity but by recognising that we need them".[22] This is reflected throughout the whole movement's structure; the twin needs of the person for autonomy and solidarity mirrored in the grassroots local action of the Emmaus communities within the wider network of mutual support. It is a partnership of equals (in an absolute sense), which upholds the truth felt deeply by Fritz Schumacher that "the really helpful things will not be done from the centre; they cannot be done by big organisations; but they can be done by the people themselves." [23]

* * *

References

P. Atohoun, Interview taken from *Nokoué: the Water Companions*, available online at www.emmaus-international.org.

R. Foreman, R. Lovatt, D. Marshall and C. Whitehead (2004) *Emmaus in the UK: Building on Success*, Emmaus UK.

I. Kougbe, Interview, Emmaus International Newsletter, December 2006.

H. Le Boursicaud (1991) *Rags to Riches: The Story of the Companions of Emmaus*, Veritas.

H. Lefebvre (1991) *Critique of Everyday Life*, Verso.

G. Lemos (2000) *Homelessness and Loneliness*, Crisis.

A. Pierre (1994) *One Earth for the Sharing* – editorials by Abbé Pierre, IME.

A. Pierre, Emmaus Cambridge website, available at www.emmauscambridge.org/opus25/Emmaus_information.pdf.

E.F. Schumacher (1974) *Small is Beautiful*, Abacus.

United Nations (2006), *Gender, Water and Sanitation: A Policy Brief*, United Nations.

Universal Manifesto of the Emmaus Movement, 1969, available at
www.emmaus.org.uk/assets/files/universal-manifesto.pdf.
A. Woodrow, Obituary of Abbé Pierre, *The Tablet*, 27 January 2007.

Notes

1. Pierre 1994, p.77.
2. Universal Manifesto of the Emmaus Movement, 1969.
3. Pierre n.d.
4. Woodrow 2007.
5. Pierre 1994, p.78.
6. Pierre 1994, p.89.
7. Pierre 1994, p.67.
8. Pierre 1994, p.60.
9. www.crisis.org.uk.
10. Lemos 2000, p.1.
11. Lemos 2000, p.13.
12. *Ibid.*
13. Schumacher 1974, p.161.
14. Le Boursicaud 1991, p.46.
15. Foreman, Lovatt, Marshall and Whitehead 2004, p.15.
16. Le Boursicaud 1991, p.108.
17. Lefebvre 1991, p.229.
18. Kougbe 2006.
19. United Nations 2006, p.3.
20. Atohoun 2007.
21. Pierre 1994, p.78.
22. Le Boursicaud 1991, p.43.
23. Schumacher 1974, p.184.

Websites

For a complete list of current and prospective communities in the UK please see the
Emmaus UK website at www.emmaus.org.uk.

For full details of Emmaus's solidarity actions and community groups around the
world please visit the Emmaus International website at
www.emmaus-international.org.

Chapter Eight

Diaspora communities: global networks and local learning

by Abdullahi Haji-Abdi and Betty Okot
with Ros Wade

Introduction

With large movements of people taking place across the globe, often as the result of global crises, Diaspora communities are growing and becoming increasingly important. These communities often confront global problems in ways which host communities do not. As a result they often face an immediate need to address 'local-global' issues and tensions.

This chapter examines the capacity to develop responses to local-global issues through the development of learning communities, based on Diaspora experiences exemplified through two case studies. The first looks at the experience of a London-based community organisation, the African Community Development Foundation (ACDF), and the second focuses on the London Somali community. The case studies will discuss the potential to bridge community divisions and build a sense of shared identity. They have been researched and written by members of Diaspora communities in London. They are also both alumni of the Education for Sustainability (EfS) programme at London South Bank University.[1]

London is home to a rich mix of migrants, and some 300 languages from all over the world are spoken in the city. Some communities are long established, others of more recent origin, and some are a mixture of the two. One of the first things migrants often do on arrival in a new place is to group together to provide mutual support and information. So it is not surprising that London with its diverse pool of migrants has become home to a vast and rich array of Diaspora community organisations.

What do we mean by Diaspora communities?

Diaspora, a Greek word, was once used in reference to the dispersion of people, but over time the term evolved encompassing meanings and various interpretations. For instance, to Africans and Jews it once suggested pain and nostalgia, but as Robin Cohen (1997) aptly puts it, "Today the term has changed again often implying a positive and ongoing relationship between migrants' homelands and their places of work and settlement."[2] This analysis reflects how language dynamics alter migrants' host-home country relationships and developmental roles overtime.

Defining Diaspora communities is not an easy task because of the numerous political, social, economical and cultural factors which interconnect with their origins and heterogeneity. In London, for example, there are several such communities of varying ethnicity, cultural heritage, nationality, race and generation, but all share a collective Diaspora bond. Among African communities, this common identity introduces a type of new multiculturalism, which could potentially transcend the boundaries of national identities and thrive on a shared sense of 'Africanness'. This notion of 'Africanness' enables complex 'intra-', 'inter-', and 'extra-Diaspora' interactions between different ethnic or national African groups and other communities which widen networks and reduce chances of encapsulation. Since the African Union (AU) recognises all Africans in the Diaspora as the 6th constituency of the AU, with equal rights to participate in Africa's development, many seem to see in this 'relationship', the dawn of a new 'African dream' – a dream in which all aspirations for a better Africa count.

All the same, Diaspora perspectives of who or what they are remain accommodating, flexible, inclusive, and supportive of self-definition, allowing those who do not necessarily identify themselves as Diaspora to opt out. Also, the term is not synonymous with race as it is applied interchangeably with the Black and Minority Ethnic (BME) concept. When used in reference to BME it is always inclusive. Hence it is always problematic to either engage with or treat the Diaspora as homogenous.

On the basis of their diversity, Diaspora participation in local-global learning networks has a great potential to contribute new learning and thinking on current development issues and challenges because many Diaspora organisations are already involved in various networks as practitioners and/or service users. Within existing networks there appears to be a growing sense of development **'in, by and through the Diaspora'**,[3] which offers opportunities for information, knowledge, skills and other forms of exchanges locally and globally.

Development 'in' the Diaspora means that there should be livelihood opportunities, for example access to employment, resources and other services to improve their lives. Development 'by' the Diaspora builds on a successful development 'in' the Diaspora to facilitate activities or programmes that promote development in host and home countries. Lastly, development 'through' the Diaspora refers to those initiatives supported 'by' or 'in' the Diaspora, which might come in the shape of projects, social and financial remittances and other developmental contributions.

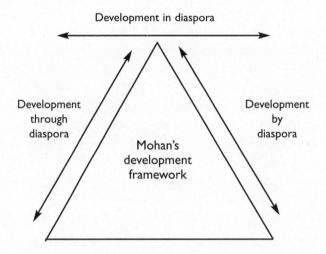

Figure 8.1: Mohan's diaspora and development framework

Towards global/local learning networks

When people migrate and settle in new environments, they often look to maintain links with their countries of origin. These links are facilitated by networks of civil society organisations (CSOs). There are several Diaspora-led or funded CSOs in the UK, working with Northern and Southern communities.

In some quarters there seems to be a growing consensus that Diaspora networks have become 'indispensable' in promoting development in poor countries because of their abilities to engage in trade, remittances, aid, migration, ideas and technology. On the basis of Mohan's framework, Diaspora participation in local-global learning networks is doubly crucial as they may enable quicker access to and transfers of relevant resources such as human and financial capital. Then again, involving the Diaspora in local-global learning networks will not be without its challenges due to certain conflicts of ideas and practices. Examples of such divergences are regular in the development sector, where Diaspora and mainstream organisations work but share little in common. But rather than concentrate on existing divisions in the sector, there might be some comfort in accepting that Diaspora concepts of development often appear to challenge grounded ideas and practices because they are moulded on flexibility, adaptability and the creativity to think and work outside known parameters. When such conflicts impact on Diaspora images, they give way to the 'politics of invisibility', which push them out of sight. The 'politics of invisibility' underscores everything in any society, from an organisation's success, image, credibility, accessibility and acceptability, to its relevance. It also underpins the labelling of Diaspora and other smaller organisations as 'hard to reach'. As the Diaspora fade from view, their culture and knowledge become less understood and increasingly ignored when the most important public debates take place. If allowed to take hold and spread, the 'politics of invisibility' limits participation beyond the immediate community.

Case Study One: African Community Development Foundation (ACDF): challenging the politics of invisibility

Founded in 1999 in the UK, ACDF [4] might appear at first sight to be just another one of the numerous smaller organisations dotting the UK civil society landscape. But on a closer look, the organisation comes into its own and projects its individuality through creative projects. Despite being small and rather invisible beyond its established networks, ACDF is no stranger to the interdependencies between local development needs and global issues. As a result it makes every endeavour to employ community development approaches to achieve its mission of improving the capabilities of individuals and community-based organisations to become active agents of change. Without doubt this organisation adds a whole new meaning to poverty alleviation by supporting self-reliance as the most effective means of improving the quality life of the poor.

Thus to fulfil its local mission for development 'in' the Diaspora, it provides advice, information and guidance (AIG) to individuals in need of practical and strategic support with solving personal problems. With its community development arm, it promotes 'intra- and inter-community' dialogue through networking, advocacy and measured community support. ACDF also facilitates training in core organisational management skills, mentoring and capacity-building. Being passionate about the integration of African Diaspora immigrants in host communities, it responds to this specific area of need by raising awareness of education, training, health and employment issues.

The organisation has already built a catalogue of achievements over the years: its track record demonstrates years of needs-driven partnership working. However, the types of collaboration ACDF engages in are rather delicate and/or cosmetic, and rarely appear to tick all the boxes of conventional partnerships. This is because in a competitive environment smaller organisations seek funds and partners with the aim of addressing pressing problems. Often, organisations like ACDF are prompted more by the need to support their client group than look for long-term relationships. It is thus less surprising that in ACDF's case some of the partnerships have been short-term or project-focused. This demonstrates that most funding agencies end up creating cosmetic relationships/partners for strategic purposes. In such cases, the partner organisation involved is funded to deliver a project which the funder might be passionate about but is incapable of undertaking.

With the aim of supporting development 'in' the Diaspora, ACDF partners with other agencies at local levels in the UK where possible. In conjunction with Cross River Partnership (CRP) in 2002/03, ACDF provided core charity management skills training, capacity-building and mentoring to African community organisations in London. Additional community capacity-building collaborations included London Borough of Lambeth Council in 2002/03, Waterloo Community Regeneration Trust (WCRT) in 2003/04 and Capital Community Foundation (formerly South East London Community Foundation) in 2004/05. All these engagements were really cosmetic partnerships, involving funders and ACDF as the delivery body.

On the other side of the spectrum, we see ACDF furthering development 'by' and 'through' the Diaspora in Africa. This aspect of the organisation's work takes on a more dynamic shape, which enables its African programmes to add value to specific international development goals. In Africa, ACDF focuses on sustainable development by localising Millennium Development Goals (MDGs) within Africa's poorest communities and strengthening the capacity of African civil society, local government agencies and businesses to become effective partners in development.

Since it is based in the UK, ACDF needs locally-based African partners to deliver. This is where the partnership spirit is put to use again to ensure cost-effectiveness and sustainability, to harness local resources, to provide local solutions to local problems, and to facilitate North-South and South-South collaborations. The ACDF approach adds a fresh meaning to development 'by' and 'through' because it creatively uses partnerships to empower the poor. In January 2007, the organisation teamed up with London-based Tax Justice Network[5] and the University of Nairobi (Kenya) in a two-day international conference on Tax, Poverty and Finance for Development. The event addressed corruption-related capital flight from Africa and highlighted fiscal probity in African countries as the best means of mobilising resources for poverty reduction. The upshot of this conference was the creation and launch on January 24th 2007 of Tax Justice Network for Africa[6] – a pan-African advocacy network – as part of the 2007 World Social Forum held in Nairobi, Kenya. The expectation was that by creating a pan-African campaign to increase fiscal prudence and economic justice, there would be increased potential to reduce poverty and improve conditions of living in most households in Africa.

At the time of writing, ACDF was in the final stages of developing a volunteering project[7] to increase the participation of African Diaspora professionals in Africa's development. The project is expected to facilitate short-term placements in Africa and encourage 'brain-gain' by addressing certain specialised professional skills shortages. ACDF expects to roll this programme out in the five East African countries of Kenya, Tanzania, Uganda, Rwanda and Burundi at different intervals. It is hoped this will encourage brain-gain and contribute to MDGs at the local levels in Africa. If all goes according to plan, the project should commence at the end of 2008 with support from Voluntary Service Overseas (VSO) and the Department for International Development (DFID).

Community self-help

Although ACDF relies on strategic partnerships to deliver, it also champions the traditional 'African' self-help ethos of development. This line of thinking argues that when involved in their own development, poor communities can take ownership, feel valued and be empowered to do more. Hence the way in which the organisation operates sheds some light on the tensions and ideological conflicts affecting Diaspora and mainstream relations. A good example of such challenges are evident in ACDF's interpretation of sustainable development. It argues that sustainable development should be an enabler, create lasting solutions with significant autonomy, and utilise readily available resources in specific communities. Inevitably, ACDF backs the thinking that sustainable development must ensure economic competence, shield and repair eco-systems while improving the well-being of all.

The self-help agenda has driven ACDF and influenced its staffing strategies since its inception. As a result the organisation has worked through volunteers from the start, despite the challenges of retention. The types of volunteer who run ACDF are highly skilled professionals from both the African Diaspora and beyond. They are mostly sourced during networking events, from self-referrals and other forms of recommendations. However, volunteer dependency creates huge staffing challenges for the organisation, as most are either employed elsewhere, pursuing further education or looking for new opportunities. It is thus apparent that volunteer mobility and funding are the greatest constraints and threat to the organisation's capacity, sustainability and skills base. At the time of this study, ACDF was beginning to rethink its staffing and volunteer retention strategies, mindful that they have survived on the passions and professionalism of volunteers. In light of this, ACDF's current profile suggests that there is room for change and organisational growth.[8]

It is possible that the passion sustaining ACDF is reinforced by the volunteers' sense of belonging to the communities they work with. These are people with experiential knowledge of local needs, who have the ability to articulate these at global-local levels and translate them into projects. However, the ACDF might have to review its emotional pillars – the volunteers and their passions – to ensure that there is enough commitment and interest to push the organisation in new directions. This will in turn influence professional thinking and commitment, and support the organisation as an agent of change aiming to empower the poor by making them self-sufficient or providing opportunities for participation. Because sustainable development can never be achieved **for** a people, it should be **by** and/or **with** them. This is where there is a stark difference between Diaspora and mainstream development responses.

ACDF seeks to promote development **with, through and by the people.**

Case Study Two: empowering the Somali Diaspora in the UK through engagement with learning for sustainability

Somali community projects have always been the first point of contact for the Somali Diaspora when they arrive in the UK. They offer opportunities for emotional and spiritual support and cultural association, general advice and practical help particularly during the first few months (Carey-Wood *et al.*, 1995, p.86). They run advocacy and information services, supplementary classes and homework support activities. They offer support to Somali children, young people and their parents, adults, women's groups and the elderly. There are more than three Somali community projects in each borough of London offering identical services and competing for funds. This complex community setting confounded local authorities and other funders when deciding how to prioritise their financial allocations to local community organisations. As a result, the Somali Diaspora in the UK became divided and isolated, with a researcher describing them as the 'invisible community'.[9] Indeed they appear to be doubly invisible, both within discussions on local development as well as in national debates about international development. Similar to other voluntary groups, Somali community projects are, as Rochester (1999) has shown, usually small charity organisations with one employed member of staff and a small number of active volunteers, having limited financial resources and generally being quite isolated. Somali community projects will have a recognised constitution and management committee and since they are a focal point that offers a significant support to Somali community members, they have the potential to be a key stakeholder that can bridge community divisions and spearhead the development of a sustainable learning community.

Somalis have been in Britain since the mid-nineteenth century. However, the biggest group arrived after the civil war started in Somalia in 1988, meaning that many are still at the stage where their experience is full of pain and nostalgia. This community has a distinctive culture and background. They are black, are culturally both Muslim and African, have distinguishing physical features, and come from a non-English-speaking country which is amongst the poorest countries in the world. It is an invisible community, and absent from local and national network meetings. Somali children often fail in schools, and there are many concerns around immigration, housing needs and health. An important issue for Somali communities is the clan/tribal difference between Somalis. Somalia is the only country in Africa whose population is composed almost entirely of one ethnic group – Somalis. They are also almost entirely Sunni Muslims. Therefore difference in terms of culture, religion, and colour is unknown in Somalia. However, they are divided into tribes, clans and sub-clans, which are based on a system that has no appreciation of difference. The clan is the basis of every Somali's identity, with loyalty to one's tribe paramount. When meeting someone for the first time, a Somali is likely to ask "Which tribe do you belong to?" rather than "Where are you from?"

The long migration movement and the hardship experienced on settlement in the UK contributed to the formation of different Somali community projects which duplicated services and efforts. It was a long migration movement: they fled from their own country and went through different countries until they arrived in the UK. That involved a life transition within a few weeks – from an underdeveloped country to a developed country where day-to-day life is much faster. They came from a world where civil war, famine, food shortage, poverty, diseases such as malaria and tuberculosis and internal displacement were the main concerns. They came to a developed world where food safety and climate change are the major concerns. It is a world where you have to get on with life. The early part of their lives in the UK included homelessness, living in temporary accommodation – often changing addresses three or four times – which also meant children changing schools several times. Sometimes there was family breakdown, leading to an increase of single mothers looking after the children and taking over the day-to-day running of family affairs; culture shock and language barriers, unemployment – with past experience not recognised, and hence low income – and lack of skills. Even the Somali community projects, which were established to support the newly arrived refugees, never had a proper community development strategy (Duke *et al.*, 1999). They were responding to the needs of the community members as they arose.

Establishing the Somali Community Forum

Given this, it was decided to establish a Somali Community Forum, which could represent Somali community projects based in each London Borough, and would facilitate the engagement of the Somali Diaspora. It was hoped that the exercise of developing the forum would also involve bridging community divisions and enhancing its communication with local and national networks. The process of engagement began by building a sense of shared identity among the Somali Diaspora through the development of a learning community around issues of sustainable development. The main challenges of this project include:

- Uniting the thinking of the Somali community projects that may lead to improving the working relationship between different Somali groups based in the same borough council

- Improving Somali community projects' relationship, initially with local authorities in which they are based, and subsequently with other potential funders that offer grants to the various Diaspora communities in the UK.

Catalysts and barriers

In early discussions, key members of Somali groups came together and identified issues which could trigger progress or present a barrier to the development of the Somali Community Forum. The catalysts include:

- The researcher's presentation had inspired co-ordinators to rethink their community leadership

- Project co-ordinators had commitment to promote the new Community Forum

- The local council would support the Community Forum initiative

- Two of the community projects presented their intention to run joint activities promoting sport within the community.

The barriers include:

- Members of new community projects were suspicious about the formation of the forum

- Members of established community projects might assume that they had the right to lead the new forum
- There was a general fear that the local council would use the forum to disempower the individual Somali community projects.

To develop the process further, it was suggested that engaging with learning for sustainability could help the co-ordinators of Somali community projects to review their skills and vision towards sustaining the Somali Diaspora in the UK.

Sustainability

Sustainability is a contested concept, and as Huckle (1996) writes, meaning is always dependent on the context in which it is used. The best-known definition comes from the Brundtland Report in 1987, which defines sustainable development as "development that meets the needs of the present without compromising the ability of future generations to meet their own needs" (WCED, 1987). While this requires the consideration of both current and future generations, the Somali community in the UK is not in a position to visualise that link, as it is still struggling to survive in the host country. Furthermore, this definition includes a time factor which links current and future generations. As a result, this community needs a new kind of education that makes it aware of sustainability and its principles. The United Nations has presented the role of education in sustainable development as "critical for promoting sustainable development and improving the capacity of the people to address environment and development issues. . . . It is also critical for achieving environmental and ethical awareness, values and attitudes, skills and behaviour consistent with sustainable development." [10]

For this reason, a more practical and appropriate sustainability model for the Somali community is one which comprises three guided principles that link economic, social and environmental components or 'capitals' (Edwards, 2005). Social capital relates the role of the community in getting retrained and equipped to understand the effects of our environmental impacts. It values the traditional knowledge and skills of community members. Economic capital refers to financial resources, and environmental capital encompasses all the resources of the earth including nature, farming and renewable energy, minus the negative impacts of pollution and desertification. Putnam (2000, p.22) presented two types of social capital which can shape the Somali community's understanding of sustainability. 'Bonding' social capital relates to community members' common identity, encouragement of community activity, participation and development of supportive community projects. 'Bridging' social capital refers to the diversity of relationships and networks existing between local and national agencies. The Improvement and Development Agency for local government (IDeA, 2002 p.12) added one more type of social capital named 'linking', which relates to ties with the local authority and participation in local network for social and political lobbying.

For the Somali communities in the UK, Education for Sustainability (EfS) means first of all reflecting on their life since their arrival in the UK – reflection on how their needs in regard to immigration, welfare, education, employment, housing and heath issues have been met. For the Somali community projects, it is about reflecting on the support offered to community members: the quality of their service, empowerment of the community members, raising the standard of refugee children's education and the promotion of cultural and religious needs. Overall it is a reflection on their life transition from Somalia to the UK, from Africa to Europe, from a Third World country to a developed country. It is also a reflection on expectations, myths and the reality of coming to the UK.

While critical reflection is the starting point of the sustainability process, the next stage leads to the building of a sustainable community. This involves learning about environmental sustainability and becoming an active participant in decision-making at community and then neighbourhood levels, empowering the Somali communities to challenge their present situations when appropriate. Community participation is paramount in achieving sustainable development (Warburton, 1998) and in many cases Somali community projects need to initiate a new kind of relationship between themselves and the local council to facilitate access to both human and financial resources available within the local area. To start this process, Somali community projects must firstly assess the programmes they currently offer and then bring together their efforts and set out a shared vision to the Somali Community Forum, which could be the basis for developing and realising their objectives. They will also need to identify those agencies which have similar objectives and can support their programmes. By this time, Somali community projects will need to have built a system of gathering information and recording achievements and problems.

The Somali Community Forum

The formation of the Somali Community Forum was a big step towards the sustainability of the Somali Diaspora and their engagement with sustainable development. It proved relevant to the targeted community projects, who responded well in practising the art of reflection and reviewing their social capital. The Somali community projects realised that they should be part of the solution, and that this could be achieved by building a good rapport with their local council. The council officer reaffirmed commitment to supporting and promoting the Somali Community Forum, and Forum members now regularly meet to share information and discuss development programmes. They agreed to prepare a SMART business plan with emphasis on sustainability as the way forward in consolidating the objectives of the Forum. A link officer from the local council and an officer of Somali origin from a local refugee network regularly attend the Forum meetings to maintain the momentum and the spirit of the community, and to contribute to the discussions. The presence of these two officers also assures local network involvement.

To sum up, the overall benefits of the Forum are:

- Partnership work between different groups either in a same London borough council or in two different boroughs in London
- Partnership work with other local agencies which support the Forum's objectives
- Creating an environment of collaboration rather than unnecessary competition for small funds
- Local authority funding can be streamlined
- Bigger, effective and inclusive programmes could be set up
- Contributing as one voice to local consultation activities
- Somali Diaspora members can become visible in local and national networks
- A joint celebration of religious festivals and cultural events
- An increased understanding of sustainability

An additional and unforeseen aspect of this initiative brought the community together in shared social activities in a celebration and acknowledgement of the richness of Somali culture. The Forum participated in the celebrations for Black History month and Refugee Week, and on both occasions the Somali Diaspora organisations presented cultural activities and prepared traditional Somali dishes. For the first time, a joint summer project was organised which involved sporting activities for Somali children and young people and day trips for the Somali families to London Zoo and Alton Towers. This summer project was funded by the local council. A joint celebration of Eid Festivals is also planned for the future.

Conclusion

These two case studies have many differences but also much in common: both put people and sustainable development at their centre, and both challenge the simplistic notion that Diaspora communities are made up of a homogenous group rather than a rich and complex mix of social, cultural and ethnic identities. They share certain experiences, such as a sense of invisibility in the host country and a lack of voice in important debates. They are also often beset with tensions and divisions, some of which they have brought with them and others that are a result of experiences in the UK.

The Somali Community Forum has increased their visibility through an improved relationship with the local authority. This in turn has had a direct impact on engagement of the Somali community with local events, and given the community a voice in local development. ACDF still struggles to be heard at national level, but has succeeded in cutting through the mainstream international development agendas to work directly through the Diaspora to find local solutions.

There is much to learn from these experiences. There will undoubtedly be a growing number of Diaspora communities around the globe in the coming decades. Some of these will be from choice, but many will be as a result of war and other global crises as the effects of peak oil and climate change become more acute. The skills which are so crucial to Diaspora communities – of adaptation, resilience, conflict resolution and self-empowerment – will be essential for all of us if we are to create a just and sustainable future for humankind.

* * *

References
J. Carey-Wood, K. Duke, V. Kam and T. Marshall (1995) *The Settlement of Refugees in Britain*, Home Office Research Study No. 141, HMSO, London.

R. Cohen (1997) *Global Diasporas: An Introduction*, University of Washington Press, Seattle.

K. Duke, R. Sales and J. Gregory (1999) 'Refugee Resettlement in Europe', in A. Bloch and C. Levy (eds.) *Refugee, Citizenship and Social Policy in Europe*, Macmillan Press Ltd, London.

B. Edwards (2005) *Rough Guide to Sustainability*, 2nd edition, RIBA Enterprises Ltd., London.

H. Harris (2004) *The Somali community in the UK: what we know and how we know it*, commissioned and published by The Information Centre about Asylum and Refugees in the UK (ICAR).

J. Huckle (1996) 'Realising Sustainability in Changing Times' in J. Huckle and S. Sterling (eds.) *Education for Sustainability*, Earthscan.

IDeA (2002) 'Social Capital, a Discussion Paper', www.idea.gov.uk/idk/core/page.do?pageId=1347434.

G. Mohan (2002) 'Diaspora and Development' in J. Robinson (ed.), *Development and the Displacement*. Oxford: OUP/ The Open University, p.104 cited in C.-E. Chikezie (2004) *Diaspora and Development: Africans Without Borders*, London. African Foundation for Development (AFFORD).R.D. Putnam (2000) *Bowling Alone: The collapse and revival of American Community*, Simon and Schuster, New York.

C. Rochester (1999) *Handbook for voluntary organisations*, Centre for Voluntary Organisation, London School of Economics and Political Science.

Notes

1. See www.lsbu.ac.uk/efs.

2. See R. Cohen 1997, University of Warwick, UK: www.transcomm.ox.ac.uk/wwwroot/global.htm for more information (last accessed 11/6/2008).

3. Figure 8.1 is based on G. Mohan (2002) 'Diaspora and Development' in J. Robinson (ed.) *Development and Displacement*, p.104. I owe this diagram to Chukwu-Emeka Chikezie of the African Foundation for Development (AFFORD), www.afford-uk.org.

4. For more information visit www.acdf.org.

5. www.taxjustice.net.

6. www.taxjustice4africa.net.

7. For more information on Diaspora and overseas volunteering, see www.dfid.gov.uk and www.vso.org.

8. I owe this observation to Alache Ode, the Diaspora and Volunteering Programme Manager, Voluntary Service Overseas (VSO), UK. See www.vso.org.uk.

9. Harris 2004, p.6.

10. UNCED, Agenda 21, Regency Press, London, 1992 (cited in Huckle *et al.* 1996 p.2).

Chapter Nine

A dose of passion: radio, research and change in Africa

by Monica Janowski and Kaz Janowski

The potential impact of using mass media, including and perhaps especially radio, to bring about change is widely recognised (e.g. see Gumucio Dagron 2001). However, this potential is not always fulfilled. We would argue that in order to make the most of mass media's ability to deliver messages, there needs to be close, hands-on collaboration between those with the message, those with the technical skills to deliver it, and potential beneficiaries of the message. This is particularly true where the content and implications of a message are complex and multi-dimensional. We want here to examine one context where this is the case – where research is linked to the message – and to examine ways in which one mass medium, radio, can be effectively brought closer to both researchers and audiences to create more effective communication and hence lead to more effective and appropriate messages relating to behavioural change.

Research, particularly technical research, is rarely 'sexy'. The knowledge it generates and the processes it involves are usually seen as a kind of medicine – necessary, but not tasty. However, we would like to argue here that through the use of mass media there is the potential for transforming what often appears to non-specialists (and sometimes even to specialists) as 'dry', tasteless and medicinal into something attractive, even something which evokes passion. We draw on the experience of two research projects, in Uganda and in Zambia, to argue that the use of radio as an inherent part of such projects can breathe life into topics, issues and processes, transforming them from something dry and technical into something full of life and accessible to all. This, we argue, can be achieved through a close and interactive relationship between researchers and radio specialists, with close reference to audiences.

Research and behavioural change

The term research covers a multitude of things, ranging from very abstract technical research to research into human behaviour. All research has, potentially, an implication for changing human behaviour, although this is not always something which researchers are directly concerned with. However, there are some contexts where the link between research and behavioural change is explicit. This is particularly true as regards research funded through international development agencies, where the rationale for funding is based on the applicability of the research, and the boundaries between research and its application become blurred. What transpires is what is called 'action research', where a project is seen as both carrying out research and attempting to bring about behavioural change. This type of project often has confused goals (despite the apparent logic of such devices as the UK Department for International Development's 'logframe') and presents a difficult task for those working on it, who are usually researchers with little understanding of how to bring about change. This particularly applies to natural scientists, who are not trained to analyse human behaviour; but it also applies to social scientists, who are often more concerned to observe *what* people are doing than trying to make them *change* their behaviour; indeed many academic social scientists are resistant to the idea that they are required to bring about change in behaviour: as far as they are concerned, that should be the job of government agencies, NGOs and community organisations. Nevertheless researchers pay lip-service to acceptance of this role, since it is a prerequisite for successfully applying for funding. However, privately they are often very frustrated and even angry at the difficult position they are put in, with insufficient experience, networks, political clout or money to bring about change.

There is, then, an inherent tension within many research projects funded through international development agencies. Researchers are tempted to deal with the requirement that they show impact by handing over this responsibility to others – to government agencies, NGOs or mass media. In order to make a clear separation between their job and the job of the agencies doing the 'disseminating', there is a tendency to want to hand over a clear-cut 'magic bullet' message, rather than engaging in a process of developing a message in its most appropriate form – or, indeed, making any alteration to the message. This is not only true of natural scientists but also of social scientists, despite their recognition that the message which they are disseminating needs to be developed through dialogue with the potential beneficiaries. Social scientists working on 'action research' projects (and on 'research' projects funded by international development agencies which are not formally termed 'action research' but which carry the requirement to show impact) tend to limit their involvement to qualitative and quantitative assessments of behaviour and do not happily become involved in transmitting the message which leads to changed behaviour.

The implication of this is that in their dealings with mass media such as radio very few researchers have shown an interest in becoming involved in the nuts and bolts of developing radio programmes, or of the possibilities of bringing radio into the design and process of projects. Mass media are generally seen as something to be used at the end of a project to transmit messages, and the job of developing the messages is handed over to media specialists.

There are problems inherent here. Media specialists lack in-depth knowledge of either the subject matter or the audience. They attempt to respond to what they perceive to be the requirements of the researchers themselves and the sponsoring agencies, and attempt to engage with the audience as far as possible. However, there is a limit in the extent to which it is possible to fulfil any of these different requirements of their 'clients'. Because of the separation between researchers and media specialists, there has been a tendency for messages to be handed over complete in themselves – magic bullets, magic medicine. This means that the message may be over-simplified, inaccurate in research terms and/or inappropriate to the social context. Researchers themselves are often not happy with the way their findings have been handled by the media; and audiences fail to respond or change their behaviour.

Another issue around the dissemination of research findings through the media is that they are often handled in a rather dry, technical way, which is difficult to understand for the non-specialist and which fails to touch the hearts and minds of the audience. In relation to certain key issues, particularly in the field of health (such as malaria and HIV-AIDS) there has been funding for much more audience-friendly use of radio, using local voices and incorporating such things as radio listening groups. However, for much research, particularly technical research, the means of transmission remains such models as used by the Developing Countries Farm Radio Network, which gathers the findings of research and sends out scripts for reading out on local radio. These are a very useful means of disseminating the scientific messages of key projects to a wider world. However, they are usually only fully comprehensible to relatively well-educated extension staff. They are also very dry, not bringing out any human stories behind the research findings, although they could potentially be used in conjunction with such stories on individual radio stations.

Bringing radio into research

One of us (MJ) is a social anthropologist, while the other (KJ) is a radio producer at the BBC World Service. MJ, as a social anthropologist, is very aware of the importance of getting to know local communities and communicating effectively with them, linking radio with an in-depth understanding of audiences, something which is increasingly being recognised among radio practitioners too (e.g. see Ilboudo 2000). We became aware of the issues described above through MJ's work with natural scientists and other social scientists on projects funded through DFID and the EU. It seemed that within projects involving natural science research in particular, there were still considerable difficulties in linking research, the media and audiences. We felt that there was a need for more direct engagement between researchers and the media, and this stimulated us in 2001 to set up a project called *In the Field*. This involved working with a range of researchers on the production of a radio series for transmission on the BBC World Service, focusing on the findings and outcomes of projects on which they had worked. We trained researchers to go out as 'barefoot reporters' to talk to people in the areas in which their projects had worked, bringing back audio material which we then worked up into programmes, linked through a script. The series focused on engaging the stories, experiences and emotions of individuals – researchers, local staff of agencies, and villagers themselves. We worked closely with the researchers in selecting excerpts from interviews and writing scripts, to ensure that the series was not only appealing and accessible but also accurate from a research point of view and from the point of view of projecting the project context and 'story'. The series was produced with an accompanying booklet and website. The series and its accompanying materials proved to be very popular among listeners round the world, to judge by the letters and emails received, and requests for the booklet. Most of the responses and requests we received were not from other researchers but from students, teachers and members of the general public, and the series was broadcast a number of times after its first broadcast in 2001. The website continues to be live (see www.nri.org/projects/InTheField/).

In the Field covers a range of topics, many of which, although seen as important by funders, researchers and policy-makers, are not usually seen as either appealing or accessible among the general public – topics such as integrated pest management (i.e. using methods other than pesticides to manage pests) and the potential for new feed for goats. However, through the human stories which were included, and the 'colour' introduced through music, sound effects and, in the website and booklet, hand-painted visuals, these topics came across as lively and appealing. *In the Field* demonstrated that it was possible to 'bring to life' topics and issues which were apparently very 'dry', and to create programmes to a standard of accessibility acceptable to the BBC, while at the same time satisfying researchers themselves. This was possible through their involvement in the process of production. They were motivated to participate in the project through their desire to communicate their passion for their subjects and their projects, a passion which shone through in the series and other materials but which needed to be carefully mediated in order to couch it in language and terms which had a meaning beyond the research (Janowski and Janowski 2002a; Janowski and Janowski 2002b). This was achieved through setting up a close and 'dialectic' partnership between researchers and media specialists in developing the series. Many researchers had had frustrating experiences previously in working with media specialists, since they felt that their projects had been misunderstood and mis-communicated. This meant that while they were keen to participate, they were sometimes wary and unsure of the process of translating their research into 'popular' language. They had difficulties of their own in communicating the messages of their projects clearly in a way which would be understood by a wider audience than other researchers. A significant amount of time was devoted to dialogue in order to overcome all of these difficulties.

Following *In the Field*, we worked on other radio series for the BBC World Service on international development topics, most linked to research projects (*The Language of Development* 2002, *Making Ends Meet* 2002, *Gathering in the Rain* 2003, *Traditional Livelihoods* 2004, *Rats!* 2005 –

see www.livelihoods.org/info/audio/audio_NRI_index.html for details and audio of most of these). We felt that we would like to try to integrate radio series into research projects on which MJ was working together with other researchers, to see if we could take the role of radio further. This was not only in the context of the remit of government radio stations to 'inform and educate', but also in the context of the mushrooming of local FM and community radio stations, especially in Africa, which have the potential to relate closely to local populations (e.g. see Moemeka 1981; Gumucio Dagron 2001). This led to the making of *Together to Market* in Uganda and *Eating out Safely* in Zambia, both as part of projects funded through DFID's Crop Post-Harvest Research Programme (CPHP), which was managed through NR International, a company jointly owned by a consortium of universities. *Together to Market* was made in conjunction with a local FM station and was eventually broadcast on a number of others; *Eating out Safely* was broadcast on Zambia National Broadcasting Corporation's Radio 2.

Projects commissioned by CPHP included some led by natural scientists and others led by social scientists. *Together to Market* was made within a project falling into the latter category, which was initially entitled 'Decentralised Market Information Service in Lira District, Uganda' but later renamed (due to the prominent role which radio came to play in the project after MJ joined the project team) 'Market Information Tools: Combining Radio and Training to Facilitate Successful Farmer Group Marketing' (referred to as 'Uganda Group Marketing' here). *Eating out Safely* was made within the Zambian part of a project led by natural scientists with the mouthful of a name 'Maximising impact of food safety knowledge of street vended and informally vended foods generated by CPHP projects in West and Southern Africa using the coalition approach and extending the approach to India' (referred to as 'Zambia Food Safety' here).

The names of the projects do not, interestingly, imply that they were research projects, but rather that they were straightforward 'development' projects. Indeed, there is a sense in which the two projects were conducted as though this were the case. There was a certain level of confusion, in practice, over what was meant by 'research' within the projects and how much space was to be devoted to research. This undoubtedly to a large extent reflects the confused mandate which the CPHP programme leaders themselves were given by DFID, which required both the achievement of behavioural change and that (somewhat secondarily) what was commissioned needed to be classed as 'research'. All of the members of the project team for the Zambia Food Safety project (except MJ) were food safety specialists, and the categorisation of the project as a research project appeared to be based on the involvement of scientific researchers *per se*, even though no scientific research as such was done as part of the project. It is not clear whether in some sense either the CPHP programme leaders or the project leader saw the project's activities promoting safer preparation of food among food vendors as involving (social scientific) research into the uptake of scientific knowledge about food safety. However, this was not explicitly recognised. The survey at the end of the project assessed changes in perception and behaviour among food vendors, but did not look beyond this to examine the processes of change involved. This would be the type of survey carried out within a 'development' project without any research element. Within the Uganda Group Marketing project (in which MJ was involved from the start) there was a more explicit acceptance that the work of the project included research into the social and economic impact of what the project was doing (a somewhat circular situation which is inherent to action research). However, there was inadequate time and money allocated to the project to allow this to be pursued very thoroughly, and therefore the status of the research element was unclear.

Both in Zambia and in Uganda we believed that radio would help to achieve the development goals of the projects concerned – safer ways of preparing and handling food in the case of the Zambia Foods project, and the formation of marketing groups in the case of the Uganda Marketing project – by creating warmer, more human communication through the telling of real-life stories through the radio. We also believed that it should be possible to incorporate radio into the fabric of the project, to enhance the research element itself by bringing about better communication between different stakeholders and between the stakeholders of the project and those who were meant to benefit from it (who were the audience of the radio series), thus allowing the form and content of the message itself to be investigated and potentially reshaped.

There are some significant differences as well as parallels between the two projects, and we hope to draw out some implications and lessons based on this. We were dealing in the two cases with very different audiences, very different levels of understanding among the audiences of the development goal, and very different broadcasting contexts. The Uganda Marketing project involved broadcast over a number of rural and small-town stations, to a defined (if pretty all-inclusive, in the areas concerned) audience of farmers who were already aware that they had a problem which they wanted to solve in relation to selling to more distant markets where prices were higher. The Zambia Food Safety project involved broadcasts over the national broadcasting station to the general public, most of whom did not realise that there were safety issues associated with food stall cleanliness, although they were concerned about this from other points of view.

'Together to Market'

The Uganda Group Marketing project as part of which the radio series *Together to Market* was made was a two-year project (1 January 2003 – 31 December 2004) which involved a package of linked activities intended to encourage farmers to form marketing groups and market together. The premise of the project was that farmers in Uganda would be more able to access more distant markets if they grouped together to form co-operative groups. This premise was based on experience elsewhere in the world, but in particular the successful formation and operation of co-operative groups in Uganda, especially the experiences of an NGO called CEDO (Community Enterprises Development Organisation) in Rakai District, which was one of the partners in the project; Fred Bikande, a CEDO trainer and luminary, provided training in Lira District as part of the project. Another partner in the project was the CGIAR research centre Foodnet, based in Kampala, and the project was linked to the Foodnet initiative to disseminate market information via radio, mobile phones and posters. A premise of this Foodnet initiative was that accessing more distant markets would be easier if farmers had access to market prices, so it fed well into the Uganda Group Marketing project and would, it was hoped, be made more feasible through our project.

Initially, before MJ became involved in the project, it was intended that the project would involve only the writing of an advice manual, together with training for farmers drawing on the manual. There was a radio element from the beginning, in the link with the Foodnet dissemination of market prices through radio, mobile phones and posters, but with the decision to make the series *Together to Market* the nature of the project was radically altered.

Our intention in making *Together to Market* was to put across 'in their own words' the stories of other farmers, in other parts of Uganda, who had experienced the difficulties, excitements and rewards of setting up and running co-operative marketing groups. We believed that this would generate a significant level of empathy and emotional understanding of what was involved in setting up groups. Given that the project was a research project, we also aimed to ask what role the use of radio played in the process. Although researching the role of radio in changing behaviour – and the role of radio in research – were not formal aims of the project (as noted above, the role of research in the project was not entirely clear), enough formal and informal assessments of the way in which radio was used were incorporated to be able to draw some conclusions about this. We will return to this shortly.

The advice manual was written by a group of marketing specialists led by Ulrich Kleih of the Natural Resources Institute, University of Greenwich; an independent marketing consultant, Peter Robbins; and Geoffrey Okoboi of Foodnet. It drew on experience in other countries in the formation of marketing co-operatives, and on the experience of Frederick Bikande, one of the co-authors, in his work over a number of years supporting group formation for CEDO in Rakai District.

Together to Market was made by a team consisting of MJ and KJ, Mr Benson Taiwo of Foodnet/Radio Lira and Mr Kai Depkat of RadioWorks / Radio Lira, working closely with other members of the project team. Radio Lira was one of the partners on the project, and the series was broadcast initially on this small privately owned station in Lira town.

The programmes are focused on personal and group stories about setting up and marketing through farmers' groups, gathered in Masindi and Rakai Districts in Uganda. They cover topics chosen jointly by the radio team and the team of marketing specialists as lending themselves to 'human stories' with successful outcomes, being of particular interest to the audience of the local radio stations on which broadcast would take place, and key to the formation of co-operative groups. These topics were also the focus of the face-to-face training in group formation and marketing carried out as part of the project.

The programmes in the series were:

1. Why form groups?
2. Why market together?
3. Getting started

4. Trust and transparency
5. Getting information about the market
6. Women and men in groups
7. Keeping going – the Kamukamu women's group
8. Money matters – the Bateganda women's group
9. Getting the size right – the Andingana farmers' group
10. A vision for the future – the Kasambiya farmers' group

Programmes in the series included excerpts of interviews carried out in the field, linked together through a script read in the studio. The original version of the series was made in English, with voice-overs of the original language excerpts. Benson Taiwo received training 'on the job' from KJ, in interviewing, the use of recording equipment and digital editing.

Benson Taiwo went on to make a Luo version of *Together to Market* in November/December 2003 for broadcast on Radio Lira. Other local radio presenters also became involved through a preparatory training session which was held in Kampala, at Foodnet, for 13 local radio presenters and producers. Through the advocacy of some of those who participated the series was translated into other languages in 2004 and 2005 and broadcast on other local stations in Uganda: Ateso by Emily Arayo of Foodnet (broadcast on Voice of Ateso in Soroti District); Lunyoro by Fred Kasozi of Foodnet/Radio Kitara (broadcast on Radio Kitara in Masindi); and Luganda and Lusoga, by Emily Arayo with the collaboration of David Kaye of Foodnet (broadcast in Jinja, Kampala and Rakai District on a variety of different FM stations). PANOS East Africa, which is based in Kampala, agreed to provide support for this work to be carried through.

The multiple roles of some of the key radio presenters and producers involved in the making and transmission of the series was important in stimulating a dialogue between specialists and the audience. Benson Taiwo was secretary of the local farmers' organisation; he gathered prices and market information in local markets for Foodnet; he was a well-known figure on the radio through his role as presenter of the Market News programme (on which market prices were broadcast, sponsored by Foodnet) and of the series Farmers' Corner, both on Radio Lira; and he was involved in training of farmers in the formation of co-operatives through the project, as part of a team including Fred Bikande, Geoffrey Okoboi of Foodnet and Cecilia Agang, an independent consultant from Lira. *Together to Market* was broadcast in English and Luo in conjunction with or as part of both of these two series a number of times in 2004. Because Benson was in contact with farmers in a number of ways and contexts, he was able to use these multiple channels to feed back into each other, making it possible to go some way to readjusting the content of the training sessions and building in discussion linked to transmission of *Together to Market* within the series Farmers' Corner. Another local radio presenter who had a multiple role was Frederick Kasozi, who was a presenter on Radio Kitara and was closely involved with the local farmers' organisation in Masindi as well as working for Foodnet as a data collector. Frederick Kasozi and Benson Taiwo were important in providing a means of setting up a dialogue on the radio involving farmers in the area.

Together to Market packages are between 6 and 10 minutes long. They are designed so that they can be played out alone, but ideally as part of a longer programme which can incorporate discussion of the topics covered, including with guests and the reading out of letters, postcards and text messages from listeners. On Radio Lira, when the series was played out as part of 'Farmers' Corner', Benson Taiwo did incorporate discussion and explanation of the topics, and in later broadcasts he was able to incorporate reading out postcards from listeners. Frederick Kasozi also incorporated discussion of the issues into the broadcast of the series on Radio Kitara.

A baseline survey of sources of information on the part of farmers and traders was carried out in early 2003, early in the project. This used both questionnaires and qualitative PRA (Participatory Rural Appraisal) discussions. Radio was found to be the most important mass medium used for information on most subjects by most people, underlining the appropriateness of using radio as part of the project. In early 2004, a monitoring survey using a questionnaire format was carried out in Lira District, during the transmission of *Together to Market* and the period during which face-to-face training was being carried out; after transmission and training was completed, between September and November 2004, an evaluation survey using qualitative PRA discussions was carried out, not only in Lira District but also in Soroti and Apac Districts, following the involvement of Appropriate Technology Uganda in the project and the translation of *Together to Market* into Ateso for broadcast through the radio station Voice of Teso.

Generally, these surveys and PRA discussions found that farmers were very positive about the series. They welcomed hearing from farmers in other areas through their own voices and stories, saying that this did indeed, as we had hoped, bring to life what it meant to form a group and run it. They asked for more series of this kind, and suggested topics. Interestingly, they said that they would like a balance between 'stories' from nearby and from far away – including from as far away as Europe, where people had parallel issues to face.

The importance of combining different media to obtain maximum communicative effectiveness came out as important, particularly in the PRA discussions. Farmers said that they found the combination of radio and training ideal, and that radio on its own was not enough. Because there was a lot of detailed experience and advice to transmit in relation to the practicalities of group formation, they felt that they benefited greatly from face-to-face training; they found many of the issues complex, and needed a forum in which they could talk them through thoroughly with someone who had experience in group formation. However, they also said that training on its own would not have brought the issues to life as radio had done. A number of respondents suggested that printed material and perhaps also video shows might also be combined with the training and the radio series. Basically, the message was that a combination of media (if we include training as a medium of communication) was best.

The surveys found that men listened to the series more than women, and this fitted in with the findings of the baseline survey – that more men than women have access to radio sets. A number of respondents in the monitoring survey suggested that radios be given to farmers' groups so that they would be able to listen together. Since many of the groups are formed by women, this would also increase access by women to radios. Although there are no nationwide or even regional figures which would enable this to be confirmed, it would appear that women make up the majority of farmers' group members in Uganda, due to the ravages of AIDS, which have hit men harder than women, and, in Lira, of the Lords Resistance Army conflict, which has led to the loss of many men. In our visit to Rakai District to gather material from successful farmers' groups for the series, we were struck when we found how many farmers' groups were formed by widows who were supporting their own and orphan children. A number of women in the surveys asked for programmes related to health and the care of children, and this was explicitly linked to the fact that they were left caring for so many children on their own.

'Eating out Safely'

The series *Eating out Safely* was made in October 2005 towards the end of a one-year project (January 2005-January 2006) which itself followed on from various CPHP-funded projects aimed at promoting the safety of informally vended food in Ghana and Zambia through the training of food vendors in markets in Lusaka. Radio was brought in as a means of further disseminating awareness of the importance of safer methods of preparing food, primarily among consumers but also among vendors who had not yet received training.

As with the making of *Together to Market*, although there was no explicit research aim associated with the involvement of radio, we were able to draw some conclusions about the potential role of radio in this kind of context from a short qualitative assessment of response among consumers and vendors during the transmission of the series, as well as through the telephone calls made to the studio as part of the broadcast.

In making *Eating out Safely* we worked with the Zambian National Broadcasting Corporation, and they were generous with their physical and staff resources. They assigned one of their producer/presenters, Rosina Mbewe, to work with KJ and MJ in the making of the series, and she was taken off other duties. Rosina, like Benson, received training 'on the job' in the use of recording and editing equipment and software from KJ, while working on the making of the series.

In planning the form and content of the series, KJ, MJ and Rosina Mbewe worked closely with researchers working on the project, particularly Dr Rodah Zulu at the National Institute for Scientific and Industrial Research (NSIR) in Lusaka. They wanted to cover a range of behavioural changes which are associated with learning about the nature of disease transmission through food. The challenge was to turn a rather dry set of topics into something which would have appeal – to humanise it, in effect. The topics selected were:

1. Response to inspectors
2. Uniforms for staff
3. Management of illness among staff
4. Personal cleanliness of staff
5. Handling of money
6. Display of food

7. Managing space
8. Disposal of waste
9. Water for customers
10. Washing utensils and plates
11. From the laboratory
12. Safe surfaces for preparation, cooking and serving

While *Together to Market* was made in a scripted format, using excerpts from interviews recorded in the field, we decided to use a less controlled format for the series *Eating out Safely*. We felt that the series needed to be even more accessible and lively in order to bring in an audience. We decided that since the audience for the series would need to be enticed in, we would recruit a celebrity to be the 'star' of the series, and we chose a well-known local singer, Angela Nyirenda.

We decided that her journey towards a clearer understanding of the food safety issues would be one which the audience would share. We took her to a lab to find out about the science of food safety, and to visit a number of food stalls whose owners had received training through the suite of projects on food safety funded through CPHP. Her journey involved not only finding out about food safety but about the owners of the stalls and their personal stories. This meant that the listener was following both Angela's journey through the lab and the markets and also the stories of those she was getting to know.

We chose a magazine format, with four elements: a short 6-10 minute package, each week following a stage in Angela's 'learning journey'; a pre-recorded drama; a studio discussion with guests and listeners who phoned in; and a quiz, with prizes for listeners. Each week, Angela's journey covered one food stall and one topic; the drama, which was focused on the happenings around a fictitious food stall, covered the same topic; and the studio discussion and quiz also covered that topic. The series of magazine programmes was transmitted on Zambia National Broadcasting Corporation's (ZNBC) Radio 2 over 12 weeks from October to December 2005.

Whilst we were not able to build in a full assessment of responses to the radio series among the general public (consumers) or vendors as part of the project, since this was not an explicit research aim of the project, we have data on this from four sources:

- A 'Knowledge, Attitudes and Practice' (KAP) questionnaire survey which was carried out by local project partners and external consultants at the end of the project, covering 224 vendors and 127 consumers, which included questions on the series

- A qualitative survey on response to the series among 25 consumers and vendors carried out by MJ and Rosina Mbewe during the period of transmission of the series
- Feedback through the calls received during the course of the programmes
- Feedback on the series from Rosina Mbewe's colleagues at ZNBC

The KAP found that among the consumers interviewed, the series was well-known and a large proportion had listened to it. Although Radio 2 was only listened to regularly by 10.9% of consumers interviewed through the KAP survey, 25% of those interviewed said that they were aware of the series and 68% of these knew the correct day and time of broadcast, indicating that they were truly aware of the series (and not just trying to please the interviewer). A large proportion of informal food vendors interviewed were also aware of the series. One-third of vendors interviewed through the KAP survey knew about it and one-quarter of vendors had listened to it. Assuming that vendors listened to Radio 2 about as often as consumers in general, this indicates a high level of awareness.

It was apparent from all sources that the series had generated a lot of debate about the topics raised. There was a lot of debate on-air as part of the programme, since callers had the opportunity of challenging official guests who had responsibilities for markets – things sometimes got quite hot in the studio! It would appear very likely from the information we have that the series started a longer-running debate on the subject of market cleanliness as well as food safety, and that it stimulated demand for higher levels of cleanliness among consumers and for training in safer food preparation practices from vendors. Indeed, the researchers at NISIR expressed some concern about getting requests for training for vendors in other cities in Zambia which they were not sure they would be able to fulfil.

The level of public interest elicited through the series *Eating out Safely* is quite an achievement; although there is no doubt that the subject of safe food and cleanliness is one which is capable of engendering debate, there was a high level of technical detail involved in what was covered which would normally be difficult to get people to pay attention to. It would seem that this success was due to two things: the varied and entertaining

nature of the way the information was put across, using a magazine format which drew on debate, drama, a quiz and Angela's 'learning journey'
packages; and the human face which was put on the issues through those
packages. From the qualitative survey and feedback from listeners on-air,
and also in the view of other producers and presenters at ZNBC, listeners
particularly liked the content and structure of the 'packages', which
allowed them to visit the markets and learn about food safety issues
through the eyes of a well-known and well-loved celebrity.

When we first took Angela to a market stall and said that she would
be eating a meal there she was quite reluctant to do so, as she felt, as do
most better-off Zambians, that market food stalls are not a nice place to
eat. This was based on a general perception that such places make you
sick. By the time we had finished making the series, Angela was very positive about eating in market stalls – at least in ones which had received
training and were implementing the food safety rules of which she now
had an understanding. She had truly made the journey which the listeners
followed. What they had followed with Angela was a real journey, and
they had been able to share it. They had also been able to share her experience of learning about the lives and stories of the stallholders whom she
visited and whose food she tasted, and to partake of her delight in the
tastiness of the food which she was served in the stalls.

The process of making the two series

The process of making the series *Together to Market* and *Eating out Safely*
was an experimental one; we developed the models in discussion with the
local broadcasters and researchers with whom we were working. Benson
Taiwo and Rosina Mbewe had an important role in deciding how issues
should be tackled and questions asked, and in putting together the programmes in the series.

In making *Together to Market*, which we made in 2004, we wanted to
move away from the usual FM radio approach, which is based on a mixture of music, talk and news. We decided to make mini-features consisting
of edited inserts from interviews gathered in the field linked together by a
script, which was the model which we had used in previous series made
for the BBC World Service. Because of the clear structure involved in a feature, it would be possible to focus on specific topics and use inserts which

exemplified points made through the script. This meant that the features could function both as mini-lessons and exemplifications of these through real-life people's experiences.

The fact that Benson Taiwo, who worked with us on making the programmes, already hosted live hour-long programmes aimed at farmers suggested the possibility of broadcasting the features as part of these. Thus we ended up with a mix of the usual FM model of live radio and a more structured and field-based element. We found that this worked well because Benson had a close relationship with the audience and was able to complement the features with further discussion and response to listeners who spoke to him directly or sent in postcards.

With *Eating out Safely* we decided on an approach which was controlled but much less structured, and what we made might be described as 'as-live' reports. It was in effect a radio version of what is sometimes done on television – following a celebrity's visit to explore something new to them. The research team with which we were working at NISIR and Rosina Mbewe strongly supported this approach, and they selected the celebrity with whom we worked. The researchers very much wanted to promote the consumption of local food through the series, through encouraging listeners to realise that market food could be safe as well as delicious, and felt that informality and a 'fun' approach was important in achieving this, as food consumption is enjoyable. Angela Nyirenda had instructions as to what she should cover in her visit to each food stall, since each report was focused on a certain topic; she had instructions to be friendly and find out about the experiences of stallholders in setting up and running the stall; and she had instructions to eat the food – but beyond that she had latitude to do this in the way she felt was most appropriate. She was given guidance during the visit as necessary by Rosina Mbewe, MJ and KJ, who shared the visit – and the food! A good deal of the visit was recorded, and the making of the as-live reports involved editing and re-ordering clips from what was recorded.

An awareness of the power of material from outside the studio for use in any context other than news is not well developed at radio stations in many parts of the world, including Africa. This is largely because the technical expertise and the equipment to allow material to be brought in and edited are absent; many producer/presenters have never been exposed to the possibility of doing this. Both small private stations like Radio Lira, with whom we worked on *Together to Market*, and state broadcasters like

ZNBC, with whom we worked on *Eating out Safely*, have problems with equipment and expertise to allow outside recordings to be made and used in making up packages. We found that the producers/presenters with whom we were working at both stations had never had experience of using field recordings to make up packages. Training is increasingly being provided for local producers and presenters in the making of features, but there are problems with sustainability, since ongoing support is important and is often not provided.

Together to Market and *Eating out Safely* linked training in the gathering of live material and its incorporation into features and other forms of pre-recorded programmes, such as the as-live report format we used for *Eating out Safely*, with research involving the use and gathering of detailed knowledge about a specific area. For both series, we not only worked closely in conjunction with researchers to identify the topics to be covered, but we relied on the research infrastructure – both human and concrete – to gather audio material.

We therefore faced not only the specific challenge of 'sexing up' dry technical material but also the more general challenge of working in partnership with local radio stations which had no experience in the techniques which can achieve this. We did not want to simply make a series and hand it over for broadcast, since not only did this not seem very 'participatory' but it would not have been very effective. We needed the participation of the radio station and the local producer/presenters working with us in order to communicate with the audience fully. Radio stations are, in a sense, living entities: they have relationships with their audiences. Producer/presenters have even more lively and dynamic relationships with the listeners who listen in to them regularly. Both of the key producer/presenters with whom we worked – Benson Taiwo in Uganda and Rosina Mbewe in Zambia – are very charismatic and effective presenters. We wanted to engage them as personalities who had significance in their own right in the process of bringing the material to life and communicating the excitement of new knowledge and behaviour to the listeners.

We therefore decided that we would need to incorporate a process of 'learning on-the-job' into the making of the two series. In Uganda, KJ offered to provide an initial training session for Benson, before we began working with Benson on the making of the series. In the event 13 people turned up for the initial training. Of these, several went on to make local language versions of *Together to Market*, but only Benson worked closely with KJ and MJ on the gathering of material, scripting and editing. In Zambia, initial informal training was provided for Rosina Mbewe before going on to work with her on planning the series together with NISIR scientists, selection and briefing of a celebrity, visits to markets and labs, and editing. No script was used in the series *Eating out Safely*; impromptu conversations between the singer Angela Nyirenda and food stall holders and others were recorded, edited and strung together with some commentary from Angela.

Tailoring the process

The role of Benson Taiwo and Rosina Mbewe illustrates the importance of tailoring the use of a mass medium like radio to the specific situation. They played a key role in the process of translating research into accessible messages which cannot be 'legislated for' beforehand. Their role went well beyond the simple making of the series. They hosted and presented the series of longer radio programmes within which the pre-recorded packages *Together to Market* and *Eating out Safely* were broadcast. In Uganda, these were pre-existing radio series for farmers; in Zambia they were specially scheduled in and were given the same title as the packages – *Eating out Safely*. Thus the role of these two individuals was key to the process of communicating the research messages – and also, arguably, contributing to the research process itself.

While one can have the aim of identifying key charismatic individuals with whom to work in making a radio series, one cannot know in advance what kind of people they will be or how exactly it will be appropriate to work with them. Such individuals already have their own reputation and standing, and this is both the foundation and a limitation on the way in which outside specialists can work with them. It is obviously vital to have respect for their ability to communicate with their listeners and to build on this, rather than having too strong a preconceived notion of how a message should be communicated.

On a more practical level, we found that there were important differences between working with a small private station in Uganda and with a state broadcaster in Zambia. Small stations tend to operate on a more hand-to-mouth basis. A small station like Radio Lira is heavily constrained by financial concerns and influenced by the need for immediate returns. They tend to rely heavily on small-scale advertising and personal notices to finance them. Small stations sometimes succeed in getting significant support from outside agencies, but most operate on a shoe-string. Such stations typically have minimal resources, both in terms of concrete things like studio space (Radio Lira's studio is a very makeshift affair with carpet on the walls) and in terms of human resources (we had great difficulty getting access to their technician, and Benson Taiwo had conflicting demands on him while he was working with us). Small stations in Africa almost always charge for airtime, and Radio Lira became a partner in the project on the basis of financial support from the project. A station like ZNBC, on the other hand, is able to look further into the future since its finances are more secure. ZNBC benefited not only from government support but from larger-scale and more predictable donor support and training; ZNBC's collaboration with the project was based on the perceived training benefits of a collaborating BBC producer, and they did not ask for any payment for airtime.

However, there are also some parallels between the two situations. In both cases there is a focus on office- and studio-based investment, rather than on investment which enables outreach and outside recording. Radio Lira and ZNBC both had only a couple of sets of microphones and DAT recorders, and these were allocated to the news teams and were not available to other producer/presenters to go out and gather material. This reflects a limited awareness on the part of the management of the station of the need for material from the field. It is difficult to know why this is, but this is an important issue which needs to be addressed through both training for staff in the use of material from outside the studio and the provision of more equipment. Recording equipment was left with both Benson Taiwo and Rosina Mbewe to enable them to continue to go out to gather material in the field. It is to be hoped that both of them will continue to be involved in using the new techniques they have learned through work on the two series, as well as the awareness of the potential of linking up with researchers who have knowledge which their audience can benefit from.

Radio and research: lessons for the future

An important generalisation about the use of radio is that one should not generalise about how it should be used – "There is no established model for participatory communication" (Gumucio Dagron 2001:33). However, our experience of working in Uganda and Zambia has led us to draw out some general lessons that we would like to pass on to others who seek to make use of radio in the research for development context.

There is growing emphasis on the importance of linking sociological and social development-related research to the use of media like radio, to ensure that radio programme-makers understand the nature of local perceptions and social processes such as processes of change (e.g. see Ishmael-Perkins 2006). However, there is less emphasis on the ways in which more technical research – both natural scientific and behavioural, but particularly the former – can be linked to radio. We would suggest that more attention be paid to the ways in which this can be done to achieve educational goals and behavioural aims in a way which interfaces effectively with local cultures and perceptions, and would make some key points.

The first point is that research and radio, far from being incompatible, can form a powerful symbiotic relationship with one another to both inform technical research programmes and to communicate the findings of research to those who are affected by these or need to implement them. Indeed, this symbiosis is essential to ensure that messages are effectively communicated, where there are educational and behavioural change objectives to the research. In order for the symbiosis to be realised, radio needs, in most cases, to be integral to research projects rather than being an 'add-on' at the final stages of research and simply a tool to disseminate a ready-made 'package' of findings. To this end, our advice would be to factor how radio might enhance research from the very early planning stages of projects.

A second point relates to the radio format used. This is relevant both to the effectiveness of communication and to practicality and portability. A series of short lively packages drawing on real voices from real people in the field telling their own stories can be used to draw the attention of the audience to a series of central points which can be drawn out through broadcast in the context of a magazine programme integrating other formats such as drama, phone-in and studio discussion. This is effective in transmitting information and in generating discussion, both within the programme and more widely in society. Such packages are also portable: they can be used by different radio stations, even in different countries. They can also be reformatted, translated and adapted to different contexts.

A final point, and an important one, is the role of charismatic 'personalities' in the successful use of radio. This is particularly important where there is a need for translation and contextualisation of technical information, to ensure that this is 'humanised' and made accessible. By such 'personalities' we mean people like Benson Taiwo and Rosina Mbewe, who wear their passion for the medium and for their audience 'on their sleeve', so that audiences – and researchers – bond with them straight away. We also mean people like Angela Nyirenda, who, through her singing, has already created a close bond with her audiences, which can be built on through radio, drawing people in through empathy. Such individuals can act as catalysts to release the unique chemistry of the relationship between broadcaster, audience and researchers. They are able to act as intermediaries between the abstractions of research and the lives of audiences.

There is, we believe, much potential for a better and deeper relationship between researchers, broadcasters and audiences. Radio's unique ability to administer 'a dose of passion' can and should be built into work with researchers investigating technical areas which are important to the lives and livelihoods of audiences. But this must be through a deep and ongoing relationship, not a brief liaison at the end of a project.

* * *

References
A. Gumucio Dagron (ed.) (2001) *Making Waves: stories of participatory communication for social change: a report to the Rockefeller Foundation*, The Rockefeller Foundation, New York.

J.-P. Ilboudo (2000) 'Prospects for rural radio in Africa: strategies to relate audience research to the participatory production of radio programmes' in *African Broadcast Cultures: Radio in Transition*. R. Fardon and G. Furniss. James Currey, Baobab and David Philip Publishers, Oxford, Harare, Cape Town and Westport, Connecticut, pp.42-71.

N. Ishmael-Perkins (2006) *Understanding Community Radio Programming: Lessons for Localising Development*. Paper presented at the World Congress on Communication for Development, Rome.

K. Janowski and M. Janowski (2002a) 'Communicating innovation: the "In the Field" project', *LEISA Magazine* 18(2), pp.22-24.

K. Janowski and M. Janowski (2002b) 'In the Field: inter-cultural communication through radio and other media' in *Voices from Phnom Penh. Development and Language: Global influences and local effects*. J. Lo Bianco. Melbourne, Language Australia Ltd, pp.221-234.

A.A. Moemeka (1981) *Local Radio: Community Education for Development*, Ahmado Bello University Press, Zaria, Nigeria.

Chapter Ten

Picturing the lives of others

by John Blewitt

Introduction

Understanding the lives of other people is intimately connected to seeing and reflecting on what they do, what they are like and what they experience. This is invariably accomplished by creating pictures. For instance, aboriginal peoples in Australia painted images of spirit people, of Macassan traders from Indonesia and of European explorers on rocks and tree bark (Morphy, 1998). John White, a water-colour artist who accompanied Walter Raleigh's expeditions to the New World in the 1580s, produced sympathetic and beautiful images of the everyday lives of indigenous peoples of Virginia but these images seemed to collude with the growing imperial project of the old world. The 'natives' and their land were presented as being ripe for settlement and commercial exploitation (Chaplin, 2007). Empire and colonialism therefore transformed image-making and intellectual curiosity into instruments of domination and subjugation. Later, picturing the lives of others became bound up with documenting racial difference as cultural inferiority. In the nineteenth century anthropologists used photography to 'scientifically' map the features of savages, and a succession of World Fairs presented living tableaux of native cultures to affirm the economic, social and cultural superiority of white civilisation. In the latter part of the twentieth century these representations were re-articulated in the promotional material of many development organisations, whose imaging emphasised the differences between people in the First and Third Worlds rather than their connections and similarities. The stress on poverty, disease, hardship, conflict and famine, although designed to secure financial and other assistance, often constructed an impression of Third World people as helpless victims or even the causes of their own hardship (Palmberg, 2001). In such a context, image-based communication as a vehicle for intercultural learning and community empowerment fell far short of the potential being generated today with the emergence of new media technologies. In other words, the global production and dissemination of images and experiences of other people via the internet is providing increasing opportunities for the participation in and sharing of social knowledge, understanding and cultural experience. Only by being able to give voice to aspirations, hopes and experiences, by picturing, seeing and understanding the lives of others, can diversity and difference become the basis for community empowerment and sustainable development.

Finding a voice

Too often the monitoring, evaluation and research undertaken by governments, development agencies and universities transform these 'voices' of others into data. People's lived-experiences become fodder for spreadsheets, graphs, tables, commentaries and academic theories. People's views and ideas become transposed into the language of academic or policy speak. Sometimes fragments, quotations and glimpses, may also find their way into the reports of journalists or the work of documentary film-makers, but the traditional media – television, film, newspapers and magazines – offer highly mediated accounts of the lives and opinions of others even though they enable these voices access to a potentially large public, global, audience. New media technologies offer opportunities of a different sort – particularly to grassroots organisations, local community groups and non-professional film-makers to communicate their experiences to others. Short 'films' made with relatively inexpensive digital equipment are frequently uploaded to the websites of major media companies, where criticism of established authorities is an important aspect of their democratic public service ethos. Britain's Channel Four (C4) is one such example.

'FourDocs', a web facility hosted by C4, offer film-makers a place to upload four-minute documentaries or send URL links to where they can be seen. To be available on the C4 site, the films must comply with the FourDocs' legal and technical standards, but C4 also offers creative and technical advice, an archive of rushes and stock footage that can be used by film-makers in their own productions together with the possibility that some films will be screened on national television. For example, Ceri-Dingle's development films on Ghana, made collectively through Chew On It productions and the educational charity Worldwrite, are technically simple, direct, investigative and powerful. In *Carry On up the NGO* and *Damned by Debt Relief*, hand-held shots of markets, streets, fishermen, and of people going about their everyday business are intercut with sequences where activists eloquently speak about NGOs and governments hindering rather than nurturing the type of development Ghanaians actually require. The picture often painted by NGOs and the mainstream media, says one activist, is that "we are unable to do things for ourselves" and that "other people know our problems better than we do". There is an alternative. In *Think Big*, Ghanaians articulate their own dreams and aspirations and demonstrate actual achievements, realising the aim that "we will not be stuck in so much dependence". These films, like the Worldwrite organisation itself, challenge assumptions and stereotypes by giving producers and consumers the opportunity to perceive the world from an alternative perspective and to connect to people from different parts of the globe. One blogger on the C4 comment board discussing *Carry on up the NGO* summed it up when he wrote:

> Brilliant film! This is groundbreaking in challenging the mainstream notion that 'well-meaning' NGOs know best. It shows people in Africa demanding industry, growth, development and shunning NGOs who instead are out to preach personal behaviour and lifestyle change, infantilising Africans, who in fact are more than capable of steering their future without Western diktat. I hope the film motivates people to support economic growth rather than counselling sessions for Africa!

FourDocs aims to encourage participation and engagement with new media communication technologies rather than raise awareness about development or similar issues. By contrast, in 2006 Christian Aid produced a 25-minute video called *Bolivia for Sale*. Presented by actor Damien Lewis, it explored the negative effects of structural adjustment policies, including utility privatisation, on the lives of poor people. Screened on Britain's digital Community Channel and available for download on Damien Lewis's own website and inevitably YouTube, *Bolivia for Sale* combines a fierce criticism of the neoliberal economic policies of the World Bank and International Monetary Fund with an equally vigorous promotion of Christian Aid's own political values and organisational goals. Likewise, the media services of the Integrated Regional Information

Networks (IRIN), part of the United Nations Office for the Co-ordination of Humanitarian Affairs, are editorially independent, although video downloads and news reports do seem to reflect the views of the United Nations or its agencies. The IRIN concentrates its news reporting, radio work and short documentary film production on a broad range of humanitarian issues in mainly sub-Saharan Africa, the Middle East and parts of Asia. These films are available on its own website, with extracts and trailers also available on YouTube and OneWorld TV.

Some IRIN films have won industry awards at the Bologna Human Rights Film Festival and Stories from the Field Film Festival, adding some weight and cultural kudos to their messages and also potentially increasing their audience reach. Many films give voice to people whose experiences illustrate or exemplify key development problems and articulate many values informing international development projects. *Slum Survivors – reality in Nairobi's Kibera* incorporates sound production techniques, a western-sounding female voice-over and a hypnotic music track accompanying striking images of poverty, destitution, hardship and emotional resilience. However, there is still a sense of the African as victim, as a needy recipient of external aid and support bravely confronting circumstances way beyond his or her control. Personalised testimony articulates this clearly.

V/O: With such high levels of unemployment many young men turn to crime as an obvious ticket out of poverty.

Many end up in prison or dead.

Leaving women like Carol to pick up the pieces.

Carol: *As I said, I'm a single parent – I'm the only one to meet the daily needs of my kids – also I'm HIV-positive.*

The biggest problem in this case of being positive is that most of the time you are very weak – you don't have enough strength to work or you don't have enough strength to meet all the daily needs that you are supposed to do.

And in this condition, to survive you have to work hard, you have to force yourself even if your body is not OK.

Source: *Slum Survivors* – extract from transcript

Ethnographic and indigenous media

Many anthropologists and ethnographers have used film, digital video, still photography and audio to produce fine-grained and sensitive studies of individuals, communities and cultures in marginalised communities and remote places. The intention is to learn more and often communicate the experiences of these others to a variety of academic, public and government audiences. Frequently, visual anthropologists and ethnographers work collaboratively and co-operatively with the indigenous subjects of their researches, sometimes providing them with access to and training in the use of audio and video equipment to tell their own stories to show what is truly important and why. The *Video in the Villages* project established in 1987 famously worked with indigenous communities in the Amazon, and clips from a number of their productions are available on Documentary Education Resources (DER) whose general aim is "to foster cross-cultural understanding through educational video and film".

More recently, Rodgers and Spitz (2007) have written of their video-messaging project with migrant communities on the South African/Mozambique border. One of their video case studies is particularly affecting. A woman named Rauletta asks to send a message home to Mozambique. She stands in front of her one-roomed mud-brick house. The video camera frames her in medium long shot. There is a pause, and then she sings of the problems she has experienced in South Africa: "I have hardship, . . . my husband has abandoned me, my child has only me. . . . in this country they kill people. . . ." The ethnographers showed Rauletta's message to her family in their home village, and filmed the tearful reactions. The video message had an effect for the ethnographers' intervention changed someone's life by connecting, empowering and bringing together. The social consequences of Rauletta's message extended far beyond her personal predicament, and as Rodgers and Spitz (2007: 31) write: "Video messaging could not obviously capture the full extent of the case but gave a unique 'window', particularly into the transnational dynamics, culture and gender politics of life on this border zone."

Somewhat different but equally effective is film editor Ross Kaufmann and New York-based photographer Zana Briski's collaboration on the Oscar-winning documentary *Born into Brothels*, first screened on the US cable channel HBO in 2005. The film focuses on a few children in Calcutta whose mothers work as prostitutes in the city's red light district. Briski gives the children cameras and teaches them the rudiments of photography so they can go off to create images of their lives and experiences. Their photographs offer a child's eye view of a seedy urban environment that is nonetheless full of life and resilience. One or two of the children demonstrate real artistic talent, and since the project their images and stories have been widely disseminated through books and exhibitions gaining additional publicity prompted by the coveted Hollywood award. Perhaps the key message of *Born into Brothels* is that art and creativity can restore and empower. As Suchitra, one of the children in the film, said, "When I have a camera in my hands I feel happy. I feel like I am learning something . . . I can be someone."

Indigenous film-makers and broadcasters such as those associated with the Central Australian Aboriginal Media Association (CAAMA) have used the media to promote the social, cultural and economic progress of aboriginal peoples, aiming to create pleasure, dignity and respect in, and for, aboriginal culture while hopefully educating the wider community in Australia about the history, experience, and diversity of aboriginal peoples. Located in Alice Springs, CAAMA Productions is the largest independent indigenous production house in Australia, making documentaries and other programmes for the aboriginal satellite channel, Imparja Television, which is totally owned and controlled by aboriginal shareholders and as such is globally unique. Some films have also been made for Channel 7, Channel 4 in London, CBC in Canada, the Australian Broadcasting Corporation (ABC), and the Special Broadcasting Service (SBS). The 52-minute documentary *Seasons* made by Steven McGregor in 2004 focuses on the life and responsibilities of Moses Nunamurdirdi, a senior custodian of the Nurmurindi people who inhabit south-east Arnhemland in the Northern Territory. These people see their whole world and history as intimately and integrally connected. Understanding the seasons, of which there are five, is essential to the Aborigines' physical survival, for their food and their culture. Although driving off-road vehicles is now an inevitable part of aboriginal life, so too is turtle hunting, storytelling and the spirit world, for the Nurmurindi people's past is their identity, even though Western civilisation is now an inevitable part of their present. For Western viewers, seeing images of giant turtles being killed and butchered is a rather disturbing but necessary learning experience, showing how remote many of us are from the source of our sustenance. In *Wirrangul Women*, a 23-minute documentary made by Jason Ramp, two elderly women, Doreen and Gladys, tell the story of their lives to the camera and to the younger members of their family who are no longer able to speak their own tribal language. Consequently Doreen and Gladys, the last fluent native speakers of Wirrangul, have helped produce story books and pronunciation guides for children in schools, but film and video can perhaps offer a more profound intervention in cultural retrieval and reproduction. Ethnographer Jennifer Deger (2006) worked in the most remote part of Arnhemland with the Yolngu people in the 1990s before satellite television and DVDs became prevalent. She writes of media technologies being used and adapted by the Yolngu to articulate their own lived experience, identity and understanding of the world to produce and reproduce local ecological knowledge and cultural imagination. For Deger these technologies do not simply mediate culture – they constitute it through the engagement of the senses and of collective ancestral memory. Of the film *Gularri,* which Deger (2006: 225-6) witnessed being made, she writes:

> When I look at the shimmering waters of Gularri, I glimpse something vital about a Yolngu way of relating-in-the-world. I see Ancestrally-charged imagery that invites eyes to look beneath the surface: to know, to be touched, and to be moved by invisible visceral connections that such seeing enables. I sense the productive play of presencing and containment that brings forth luminous and powerful Ancestral truths while simultaneously conserving them. I experience something palpable about the possibilities of a vital and enduring source of insight and identity that invites and encompasses individual perceptual subjects into a wider matrix of belonging and shared meaning.

Using drama

In Canada during 2002, the television drama series *Moccasin Flats* originated in a single 24-minute production which was part of an aboriginal empowerment project, repREZentin, run by a Toronto-based company Big Soul Productions. It focuses on the lives of aboriginal young people in north-central Regina in the province of Saskatchewan. Receiving critical acclaim and having been nominated for a Gemini television award, the drama, shown both on the Aboriginal Peoples Television Network (APTN) and Showcase Television, addresses issues of urban poverty, drugs, decay, racism, masculine posturing and violence, which seem to characterise many Canadians' perception of Regina and First Nation peoples without realising they are twin products of globalisation and colonialism. With its rap and hip-hop styling, *Moccasin Flats* shows Canadian aboriginal youth expressing themselves through a hybridised African-American culture that is also deeply rooted in their own locality and lived experience. As Christine Ramsay (2005:8) writes,

> We need texts that represent the poor from their own perspective, and that show you can live with integrity and dignity in the midst of poverty. And that is exactly the achievement of *Moccasin Flats*.

Other film makers such as the well-known British documentarist Nick Broomfield have used non-fiction drama to explore equally prescient issues. *Ghosts* (Broomfield, 2006) tells the story of migrant workers from China living, working and ultimately dying in England. It is an emblematic story which, similarly to Michael Winterbottom's *In This World* (GB 2003), deals with the human devastation that globalisation, labour mobility, economic hardship, illegal immigration and human trafficking entails. *Ghosts* follows the attempts of a young single mother, Ai Qin Lin, from the Fujian province of China, who finds it impossible financially to care for her young child in the way she would wish. Leaving the child with her mother she pays smugglers of human cargo to take her to a land where she can find good and profitable work. She embarks on a six-month journey across Asia and Europe, only to find herself at the mercy of an employment agency which takes bribes in return for securing low-paid, low-status, employment for 'illegals'. She lives in appallingly overcrowded conditions with 11 other young 'illegals' owned by a white (hence ghost) shaven-headed landlord who moans about not being able to rent out space to a further four illegals. He needs the rent money.

Factory work is low-paid and dispiriting. Relentlessly, supplies of plucked chickens arrive via an overhead conveyer belt to be cut up and packed for one of Britain's major supermarkets. The cost of cheap food becomes all too apparent, and is emphasised in two vivid scenes. The first has the young mother shopping for food with a friend in a local supermarket. She picks up a pack of spring onions and remarks that although she probably picked them she can't afford to buy them. In another, after picking the apples we see the orchard being bulldozed and the trees burned. It is obviously cheaper to import apples from overseas than to source them at home, even when employing low-paid immigrant labour. Later, the Chinese workers find themselves in Lancashire where they scrape cockles from the tidal mudflats of Morecambe Sands. Following attacks from local ghosts, resenting competition from foreign workers, they are forced to work only at night. One evening with the weather bad and the tide swiftly rushing in unnoticed, the Chinese cockle-pickers become stranded and in mortal danger. In 2004, 23 Chinese workers were actually drowned and *Ghosts* is a testimony to them and the blind economic forces that caused their deaths.

Documenting urban violence and community leadership

Half the world's population now lives in cities, and street kids have become a highly visible symbol of unsustainable development. *El Banate Dol* directed by Tahani Rached (Egypt 2006) is an observational study of the strategies used by a group of young women to survive on the frequently dangerous streets of Cairo where threats of rape, kidnappings and abuse come from the police as well as other street dwellers. The film shows a devout Muslim woman, Hind, talking with and offering practical help to the girls despite the various religious taboos and social obstacles. Violence – sometimes public, often domestic, frequently drug-related – is a serious problem in many major world cities and although it affects all citizens, it is undoubtedly the poor who suffer most. The wealthier sections of the population may increasingly have to deal with property-related or economically motivated crime, but it is the low-income communities, especially in Latin America, where homicide rates are highest. News reports and documentaries such as *Bus 174* and feature films such as *Pixote*, *City of God* and *Rosario Tijeras* have brought the issues of urban violence, drug-related crime and police corruption to global audiences even if there has been some misrepresentation, romanticising and sensationalism. The hip-hop artist Snoop Dog used the favelas in Rio as the violent and sexualised backdrop for the video promo for his song 'Beautiful'. However, popular music, film and television drama often do enable urban dwellers to make sense of their experiences, maybe even inspiring some resistance and action (Benavides, 2008). Sen (2007) writes of Bollywood star Hrithik Roshan after his debut feature *Kaho Na Pyar Hai* (2000) becoming a role model for young urban males in Mumbai and

Godmother, a story of gender empowerment through revenge, was highly popular among right-wing Hindu Shiv Sena women despite a Muslim actress, Shabana Azmi, taking the lead role. Other Hindi films such as *Army* (1996) and *Gang* (2000) are powerful tales of urban violence and social revenge.

Other film projects have focused explicitly on intercultural education, communication and community leadership initiatives, and have helped nurture their development in actual conflict zones. *Promises* (Goldberg and Shapiro, 2003) explores the possibility of peace and reconciliation between Israeli and Palestinian young people living in the West Bank. *Favela Rising* (Zimbalist, 2005) shows how community leadership necessarily involves dialogue, group facilitation, conflict negotiation and inspiration symbolised by the action and energy of a single individual, group or cultural initiative. In the favelas of Rio de Janeiro, where gun crime and drug-trafficking has blighted many poor communities and distorted the life chances of many young people, the activist Anderson Sá, himself a former drug-trafficker turned musician, has become a leader of a cultural and social movement based around music – the community-based 'Grupo Cultural AfroReggae – GCAR'. The group opened its first Núcleo Comunitário de Cultura ('Culture Community Centre') in a slum area called Vigário Geral favela in 1993, and quickly organised workshops in dance, percussion, garbage recycling, soccer and capoeira (a combination of martial arts and dance). Four years later, AfroReggae opened Centro Cultural AfroReggae Vigário Legal ('Vigário Legal AfroReggae Cultural Centre'), which had better facilities to run social, educational and cultural programmes, and the vibrant hip-hop sounds of the Banda AfroReggae inspired many young favela residents to participate in the Centre, which soon offered previously unknown possibilities for collective engagement and individual and group creativity. AfroReggae has since mobilised and empowered many slum communities. In *Favela Rising*, Anderson Sá can be seen reasoning with street kids, organising events and community actions, performing his music and bravely recovering from serious injury. The film, together with the book *Culture is Our Weapon* (Neate and Platt, 2006), explores how leadership is complex, social but also intensely personal. AfroReggae and the street kids of Rio would not respond to managerial or bureaucratic target-driven initiatives, for only something truly emerging from their own lived experiences will resonate with their needs and desires for a life cleared of the false and temporary excitements of drugs, violence and macho aggression. Anderson Sá personalises and personifies the possibility and reality of change, community empowerment, leadership and sustainability.

Participatory communication

Although *Promises* and *Favela Rising* inspire and succeed because of the co-operation of their subjects, these films are in the final instance professional media products. In *Making Waves: Stories of Participatory Communication for Social Change,* a large collection of case studies produced for the Rockefeller Foundation, Gumucio Dagron (2001) demonstrates that effective communication creates bonds between localities and groups, often serving as a foundation for collective action. Although there is no one ideal model for participatory communication, common characteristics may be derived from the many practical communication projects developed over the years. Participatory communication, must always address issues of:

- **Power:** The democratisation of communication cuts through the issue of power. A participatory approach attempts to put decision-making in the hands of the people. It consolidates the capability of communities to present their own ideas about development to professional development planners and technical staff. Within the community itself, it favours the strengthening of internal democratic processes.

- **Identity.** Especially in communities that have been marginalised, repressed or simply neglected, participatory communication helps to install cultural pride and self-esteem. It reinforces the social fabric through strengthening local and indigenous forms of organisation and by protecting tradition and cultural values while facilitating the integration of new developments.

The main elements characterising participatory communication relate to its involvement of people in social change. One important theoretical framework for this owes much to radical educator Paulo Freire, whose *Pedagogy of the Oppressed* (Freire, 1972) articulates the concepts of 'conscientisation' and praxis whereby individual and groups achieve a deeper understanding of their socio-economic and cultural environments that shape their lives by engaging in action informed by the values of justice, respect, dialogue and co-operation. As seen in the earlier chapters by Cletus Babu and G. Nagarajan, this in turn develops people's capacity to transform their social worlds. Freire's lifelong insistence on situating educational activity in the lived experience of people created many possibilities and stimulated many ideas whereby informal educators, communicators and media practitioners can approach sustainable community development. Participatory video (and radio)[1] activities can mobilise, inform and disseminate information and experiences sometimes allowing people in various localities "to become actual communities, creating social ties as strong as those shared, for instance by culturally bound groups" (Madrid, 2002: 59). This is achieved because, as White (2003: 70) notes, video can entertain and act as a:

- Reflector of reality
- Facilitator of horizontal communication
- Promoter of visual literacy as a functional literacy
- Facilitator of shared experience and discussion
- Initiator of community actualisation
- Source of power

Mary Jo Dudley (2003) shows how low-cost video technologies can uncover injustices, make wrongdoing visible, question authority and bring power elites to public account by communicating alternative points of view and different moral values which simultaneously empower individuals, groups and communities through increasing self-esteem and confidence. Organisations such as the UK/French-based Insight has pioneered the use of participatory video (PV) in a number of development projects around the world, believing that as PV methods value local knowledge they can constructively connect communities with decision-makers. PV enables community members to engage with other worlds by enhancing their capacity to communicate with each other, for like so much else in indigenous culture, video is primarily a visual and verbal medium. It can reach children, the elderly and the non-literate in equal measure. "As with stories," writes Lunch (2007:31), "video helps to connect people to the reality on the ground. There is also a human connection that comes from seeing someone speak, even if it is on video."

Black Flags in Dharavi, available on the website of Shack/Slum Dwellers International, shows the residents of Mumbai's largest slum working, trading, living and most importantly protesting against the lack of consultation from the city government in a planned redevelopment of their communities. The protesters do not want to stop the development as such, but they do want to participate in and influence the form it will take, thereby establishing some control over the political decision-making process that is shaping their lived experience and livelihoods. The video is simple and direct – a determined voice-over accompanying a montage of images taken with a hand-held camera. Similarly, the labour organisation, SEWA (Self Employed Women's Association), based in Gujarat in India, trains its members to produce videos for training and advocacy purposes. Its productions have been shown in Delhi and Washington DC, and in 2002 VideoSEWA formed a co-operative with three main objectives, to:

- Promote the services offered by Sewa like healthcare and childcare and to raise awareness and develop the capacity of women workers to be more self-reliant in the face of discrimination, low income and prejudice
- Provide information and guidance related to different types of work
- Use video to help develop women leaders in various activities like making financial savings and developing business-related activities.

In bringing to view the experiences of others, video can invite viewer reflection and discussion that may help them make sense of their own reality in ways that had previously eluded them. In this way, the viewing experience raises awareness and fashions learning opportunities which aim to empathise with others or encourage a different type of thinking that relates to a functional literacy that empowers and motivates. Bery (2003: 110) notes that as a visual medium, video can be particularly powerful. Using a SEWA programme seeking to teach women the importance of being counted in the census, she writes,

> Traditionally home-based work was not considered 'work', and thus an entire economic sector was undercounted. The video, which was broadcast on local television and shown in many communities, reached out to women and their families and encouraged them to take political action – to make their voices heard in the greater community. In addition, the video and the association with SEWA validated their work and gave them the confidence and collective strength to negotiate for better working conditions.

Also in India, the global social media network Channel 19 presents the work of six Community Video Units (CVUs) who produce 30-minute 'Video News Magazines', screening them every month on widescreen LCD projectors to the inhabitants of slums and villages. Everything produced is shot, edited and scripted by 40 Community Video Producers, with topics chosen by local Community Editorial Boards rather than by external development experts. Importantly, the videos offer solutions to important community issues that need action. At the time of writing, the Channel 19 network of grassroots Community Video Producers is composed of 25% Muslim, 25% Dalit, 25% Tribal, 60% of whom are women, so giving voice to many marginalised groups. By the beginning of 2008, Channel 19 had trained 64 Community Video Producers working in 150 villages and urban slums, producing more than 40 films with over 600 screenings to 120,000 people. Two of these are promotional shorts about the work of Sakshi Media and Manyam Praja Video. The promo for Sakshi Media shows how community video addresses the aftermath of communal violence between Hindus and Muslims in the city of Panchmahal in Gujarat. It has an energetic soundtrack, and uses some sharp editing to present both men and women talking frankly about their experiences. The film-makers argue that the best way to promote peace and religious tolerance is by making documentaries in the actual language of local communities but about issues of common concern like education, health and human rights. The CVU Manyam Praja Video works with tribal peoples in Andhra Pradesh to make films on topics as diverse as malaria and the ancient culture and traditions of the area. No buses can reach these villages, no newspapers can be delivered, and to all intents and purposes the remote settlements are cut off from the rest of India, their government and the wider world. Village screenings are usually followed by discussion, questions, comments and ideas for action. The films enable villagers, dispersed across the region, to learn about each other's problems and their democratic rights to seek improvements from government. The ten members of the Manyam Praja Community Video Unit clearly believe the media is a force for changing social behaviour, attitudes and values. As one female interviewee, standing next to a group of six children, states: "The media can be useful – other villages will come to know what is happening in this village. Non-tribals will also come to know the conditions in which we live."

Creating a global public sphere

The countless video projects, photographic exhibitions, documentary films, internet resources and computer facilities to make, view, comment, discuss, share and connect ideas and experiences are arguably creating a global public sphere. This sphere, or perhaps cultural space, offers a potential for intercultural learning through communication providing the possibility for seeing the world through others' eyes or using our own eyes to see the world inhabited by others. New possibilities are being created whereby we can know ourselves, our relationships and conflicts, our similarities and differences, our own selves and our social and ecological environments.[2] Although access to this sphere is not yet available to every citizen on the planet, the new mediascape is multidimensional and polycentric, in which many different messages and opinions can be formed and communicated widely. There is no longer one major controller or producer of words and images, but rather, as the anthropologist Arjun Appadurai (1996:31) writes, a multifaceted transnational formation of imaginary landscapes, where a new role for the human imagination in social life encompassing the mechanical production of images, the fashioning of imagined communities and "a constructed landscape of collective aspirations . . . mediated through the complex prism of modern media" is in formation.

There is, however, a significant digital divide which can be cut along class, gender, ethnic, spatial and many other lines. Governments and corporations can, and do, restrict the democratic potential of the world wide web which its inventor, Sir Tim Berners-Lee, saw as its essence; but nonetheless new media technologies do create opportunities, shaping the experience and consciousness of our everyday lives in a simultaneously global and local fashion. The social theorist Anthony Giddens (1991: 187-88) puts it this way:

> Everyone still continues to live a local life, and the constraints of the body ensure that all individuals, at every moment, are contextually situated in time and space. Yet the transformations of place, and the intrusion of distance in local activities, combined with the centrality of mediated experience, radically change what the 'world' actually is. . . . All individuals actively, although by no means always in a conscious way, selectively incorporate many elements of mediated experience into their day-to-day conduct.

People select what they see or read, sometimes avoiding what is disturbing and sometimes being fired up by it but, as Giddens argues, even for the most prejudiced and narrow-minded person, regularised day-to-day contact with the world beyond is a "positive appropriation". We may all live local lives, but the world of our experiences is now truly global, and some media projects like Live Aid, Live Eight, Earth Day, Live Earth and Pangeaday reinforce this. The internet-based Panos Network, for example, is a global organisation of independent institutes aiming to foster free speech and democratic pluralism. Panos London promotes the participation of poor and marginalised people in national and international development debates through media projects that often focus on the recording and dissemination of oral testimony and organising media-training in developing countries. Pangeaday, the first of which took place on 10 May 2008, was initiated by Arab-American documentary film-maker, Jehane Noujaim, whose film *Control Room* (USA, 2004) about media coverage of the second Gulf War, and particularly the work of Al Jazeera, graphically demonstrated how different eyes, and different media, perceive the same major global event as if they were looking at different things. Jehane Noujaim's idea was to use film and the global distribution afforded by satellite television and the internet to screen simultaneously a number of short films throughout the world with video conference facilities set up in Cairo, Kigali, London, Los Angeles, Mumbai and Rio de Janeiro. Various short dramas, animations and documentaries aimed to bring the world together by using the media to engender mutual respect and understanding. As the organisers stated,

> In a world where people are often divided by borders, difference, and conflict, it's easy to lose sight of what we all have in common. Pangea Day seeks to overcome that – to help people see themselves in others – through the power of film.

Film, photography and video are very powerful media. They are never purely or simply visual. They frequently engage a person's whole being, for although we may use our eyes to see, many videos and films may also strike us between them. Zeina Aboul Hosn's poignant and personal diary, *I Remember Lebanon,* shows how most Lebanese people were beginning to engage with their national past and slowly anticipating a more peaceful and long-lasting future after experiencing a devastating civil war. Much of the film was shot in Beirut a week before the bombs started to fall once more in 2007. *Moving Windmills,* by 'm ss ng p eces', a video production company specialising in online distribution, tells the story of William Kamkwmamba, a young man from Malawi who, having dropped out of high school for financial reasons, decides to build a windmill to generate electricity for his family home in a remote rural village. He was inspired after seeing a picture of a windmill in a school textbook. Using found materials such as a broken bicycle, tractor fan, melted plastic pipes, bamboo and used copper wires, William eventually builds a series of windmills which change his and his family's life. The film ends with the young man about to study in the US in order to return to Malawi to build many more powerful windmills. The economist Amartya Sen (Sen, 1999) sees development as being attempts by individuals to realise practically those political, economic and social freedoms that will enable them to live the lives they truly value. Perhaps the most important freedom is one that allows communication and dialogue to flourish, so enabling us to picture the lives of others and to see aspects of ourselves in them.

* * *

References

A. Appadurai (1996) *Modernity at Large: Cultural Dimensions of Globalisation,* University of Minnesota Press, Minneapolis.

O.H. Benavides (2008) *Drugs, Thugs and Divas: Telenovelas and Narco-dramas in Latin America*, University of Texas Press, Austin.

R. Bery (2003) 'Participatory Video that Empowers' in S.A. White (ed.) *Participatory Video: Images that Transform and Empower*, Sage, New Delhi.

J.E. Chaplin (2007) 'Roanoke "Counterfeited According to the Truth"' in K. Sloan (ed.) *New World: England's first view of America*, British Museum Press, London.

B.A. Conklin (1997) Body Paint, Feathers, and VCRs: Aesthetics and Authenticity in Amazonian Activism. *American Ethnologist*, Vol.24 No.4, pp.711-737.

B. Cooke and U. Kothari (eds.) (2001) *Participation: the new tyranny?*, Zed Books, London.

J. Deger (2006) *Shimmering Screens: Making Media in an Aboriginal Community*, University of Minnesota Press, Minneapolis.

M.J. Dudley (2003) 'The Transformative Power of Video: Ideas, Images, Processes and Outcomes' in S.A. White (ed.) *Participatory Video: Images that Transform and Empower*, Sage, New Delhi.

P. Freire (1972) *Pedagogy of the Oppressed*, Penguin, Harmondsworth, Ch.3.

A. Giddens (1991) *Modernity and Self-Identity: Self and Society in the Late Modern Age*, Polity Press, Cambridge.

A. Gumucio Dagron (2001) *Making Waves: Stories of Participatory Communication for Social Change*. Available at www.communicationforsocialchange.org/pdf/making_waves.pdf

C. Lunch (2007) 'The Most Significant Change: using participatory video for monitoring and evaluation', *Participatory Learning and Action*, Vol.56, No.1.

N.V. Madrid (2002) 'The Role of Communication in Urban Communities' in C. Gandelsonas (ed.) (2002) *Communicating for Development: experience from the urban environment*, ITDG Publishing, London.

H. Morphy (1998) *Aboriginal Art*, Phaidon Press, London.

P. Neate and D. Platt (2006) *Culture Is Our Weapon: AfroReggae in the Favelas of Rio*, London, Latin American Bureau.

M. Palmberg (ed.) (2001) *Encounter Images in the Meetings Between Africa and Europe*. Nordiska Afrikainstitutet, Uppsala.

C. Ramsay (2005) *Moccasin Flats*: A Landmark in Canadian Television and Canadian Identity. Paper delivered to *First Nations – First Thoughts Conference*, University of Edinburgh. Available at: www.cst.ed.ac.uk/2005conference/papers/Ramsay_paper.pdf

G. Rodgers and A. Spitz (2007) 'Video Messaging in Contexts of Forced Migration: "Amplifying" Social Relatedness across Mozambique/South Africa Border' in A. Grossman and A. O'Brien (eds.) *Projecting Migration: Transcultural Documentary Practice*, Wallflower Press, London.

A. Sen (1999) *Development as Freedom*, Oxford University Press, Oxford.

A. Sen (2007) *Shiv Sena Women: violence and communalism in a Bombay Slum*, Hurst and Co., London.

S.A. White (2003) 'Participatory Video: A Process that Transforms Self and the Other' in S.A. White (ed.) *Participatory Video: Images that Transform and Empower*. Sage, New Delhi.

Notes

1. See Chapter Nine by Monica and Kaz Janowski in this book.

2. Donna Ladkin suggests something similar in her discussion of 'dwelling' in Chapter Six of this volume.

Web

Pangeaday, www.pangeaday.org.

Video in the Villages, www.der.org/films/video-in-the-villages-presents-itself.html.

Born into Brothels, www.kids-with-cameras.org/bornintobrothels.

FourDocs, www.channel4.com/fourdocs/film/film-detail.jsp?id=13321.

IRIN Film and TV, www.irinnews.org/filmtv.aspx.

INDIA: Black Flags in Dharavi, www.sdinet.org/galleries/india_video.html

Insight http://insightshare.org/#.

Community Video Channel 19, http://ch19.org/.

VideoSEWA, www.videosewa.org/aboutus.htm.

Index

Page numbers in *italics* refer to figures and tables

The SCHUMACHER BRIEFINGS series

Published by Green Books: see www.greenbooks.co.uk for more details
For details of the Schumacher Society, see www.schumacher.org.uk

REKINDLING COMMUNITY

Connecting people, environment
and spirituality

Alastair McIntosh

Schumacher Briefing No. 15

Climate change, species extinction, war and alienation. These are just some of the threats that imperil a world that gives us life. There is no single solution, but one thing is certain. Unless humanity learns how to rekindle community, all other efforts will wither on the vine.

This timely new Schumacher Briefing explores three integrated pillars of community – with one another, with the natural environment and with the spiritual ground of all being. McIntosh draws not just on his own extensive experience, but also on the work of a dozen associates at the Centre for Human Ecology – mostly his former students. These have carried out research into the spirituality of community regeneration, assisted by WWF International. Each of them provides a summary of their findings, weaving a rich tapestry that illustrates community.

With an emphasis on spirituality, the Briefing examines the implications of living as if all life is interconnected. It addresses both the theory of community and its practical regeneration. The contexts range from remote islands to inner city deprivation and even the world of corporations and government. The results fortify our capacity to face the future and point to ever-deeper meanings of love.

The Author: Alastair McIntosh is Visiting Professor of Human Ecology at the Department of Geography and Sociology, University of Strathclyde, and holds fellowships at the Centre for Human Ecology, the Schumacher Society and the Academy for Irish Cultural Heritages at the University of Ulster. His books include the bestselling *Soil and Soul, Love and Revolution* (collected poetry), and most recently *Hell and High Water: Climate Change, Hope and the Human Condition.*

ISBN 978 1 900322 38 6   96pp with b&w photos   £8.00 pb

For a complete list of Schumacher Briefings, see previous page

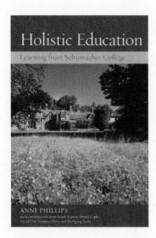

HOLISTIC EDUCATION

Learning from Schumacher College

Anne Phillips

**with contributions from Satish Kumar,
Fritjof Capra, David Orr, Vandana Shiva
and Wolfgang Sachs**

Schumacher College, set up as an international centre for ecological and spiritual studies, has developed a worldwide reputation for the quality of the unique learning experience it offers. Individuals and groups come from across the world to learn about subjects relating to environmental and social sustainability.

Students are often so inspired that many express a wish to set up similar organisations elsewhere in the world. Educators and trainers ask how the College was set up, what the magic ingredients were, and what students have done after been there. This book is an attempt to answer those questions, and describes how the College came to be set up by The Dartington Hall Trust in Devon, England. It explains the policies and practices adopted to ensure that the learning processes were consistent with – and reinforced – the topics being studied. It includes examples of what former students have gone on to do, and reflections on the College by visiting teachers including Fritjof Capra, Vandana Shiva, Wolfgang Sachs and David Orr. *Holistic Education: learning from Schumacher College* could be used as a guide to design a place of holistic learning: the key is to remember the ecological principle of context, and to apply liberal doses of local wisdom.

The Author: Anne Phillips, Director of Schumacher College from 1993 to 2006, was project manager of the group that planned the College. Her interest in how people learn developed while she was at university, and since then she has been involved in educational design with educators and trainers. She worked as a teacher in Uganda with VSO, taught at Dartington Hall School, and was involved over twenty-five years in academic and vocational curriculum development with The Dartington Hall Trust.

ISBN 978 1 900322 36 2   144pp with 16pp photos   £9.95 pb

For our complete list of books, see www.greenbooks.co.uk

Also available from Green Books

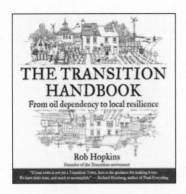

THE TRANSITION HANDBOOK

From oil dependency
to local resilience

Rob Hopkins

"If your town is not yet a Transition Town, here is guidance for making it one. We have little time, and much to accomplish."
– Richard Heinberg, author of *Power Down*

"This DIY manual for change is an intelligent and practical attempt to encourage people to think globally while acting locally."
– P. D. Smith, *The Guardian*

We live in an oil-dependent world, and have got to this level of dependency in a very short space of time, using vast reserves of oil in the process without planning for when the supply is not so plentiful. Most people don't want to think about what happens when the oil runs out (or becomes prohibitively expensive), but *The Transition Handbook* shows how the inevitable and profound changes ahead can have a positive effect. They can lead to the rebirth of local communities, which will generate their own fuel, food and housing. They can encourage the development of local currencies, to keep money in the local area. They can unleash a local 'skilling-up', so that people take back control over their lives.

The Transition Handbook clearly shows the immediacy of the need to deal with the twin challenges of peak oil and climate change. It is also a manual which will guide communities to begin their 'energy descent' journey. The argument is upbeat and positive, as well as utterly convincing.

The Author: Rob Hopkins, founder of the Transition Network, has long been aware of the implications of our oil-dependent status, and has been energetically campaigning to increase awareness of its impact, having successfully created an Energy Descent Plan for Kinsale in Ireland which was later adopted as policy by the town council. He is co-ordinator of the Transition Network.

ISBN 978 1 900322 18 8   240pp in two colours   £12.95 pb

For our complete list of books, see www.greenbooks.co.uk